ON STIEG LARSSON

ON STIEG LARSSON

Translated from the Swedish by
Laurie Thompson

ALFRED A. KNOPF   NEW YORK   2010

CONTENTS

Stieg   1
Jonas Sundberg

Working with Stieg Larsson   9
Eva Gedin

The Larsson–Norstedts e-mail exchange   23

Stieg Larsson: The Un-Swedish Author   53
John-Henri Holmberg

The Stieg Larsson Phenomenon   79
Svante Weyler

ON STIEG LARSSON

STIEG

Jonas Sundberg

Towards the end of the 1980s I became increasingly concerned with the rising tide of far-right extremism in Sweden. It had been more or less non-existent since the Second World War, until a group of fairly young people – nearly all of them men – founded an organization based on hatred against non-European immigrants. This was a new concept in Swedish politics and – although widely neglected by the media at first – it was gathering strength at the end of the 1980s.

Back then, most of those who tried to map the extreme right were doing so in their spare time. An increasing frustration over the lack of published studies was felt, but two books then appeared, giving impetus to further studies. One was a doctoral dissertation, written by Heléne Lööw, which gave a very interesting perspective back to the thirties and forties. The other one was a presentation of contemporary far-right extremism in Sweden and in Europe, written by two journalists, Stieg Larsson and Anna-Lena Lodenius. The book, published in 1991 and entitled *Extremhögern* (The Extreme Right), proved to be extremely useful and very soon became the reference on the subject. I devoured it and felt a need to talk to the authors.

Stieg received me at his office at the T.T. news agency in central Stockholm, where he was working at the time. He had a hint of an accent from northern Sweden and seemed a little reserved. However, glancing through my copy of the book with all the underlining, he saw a friend. And I thrived sitting there with him, marvelling at his vast knowledge and understanding that a real network against the extreme right was about to be shaped. I found him very humble, yet aware of the quality of his own knowledge and brilliant thinking, peering at me through his round glasses. From then on I was in regular contact with him, mostly over the telephone, but sometimes at his office or in his home. Seeing him in his home more than anything revealed how rigorous he was about his own security. He had made serious arrangements to conceal his address and to prevent assaults. One unwritten rule that was applied, even before *Expo* was founded, was that no pictures were to be taken of people within the network, which explains why today there are relatively few pictures of Stieg.

I would say that Stieg and Anna-Lena's book meant a lot for the now-emerging network of researchers on the topic. These people were disparate, but Stieg was eager to tie links with all of them, Swedes as well as people from abroad. The loosely knit-together network began to hold conferences, where people spoke of a need to organize a mapping of the extreme right and to publicize their findings. It was at one of these meetings that I became more aware of the risks involved, especially when Stieg showed a few of us a 9-mm bullet that he had received in the post. I later learned more about his simple – but intelligent – ways of maintaining a low profile.

These were days when computers and the Internet were far from being every man's tool, whichever side you were on. Hence much of the information we were looking for appeared around right extremist marches and events, and Stieg was always willing to teach others how to get to it. This was also true when it came to any sort of information or know-how. Stieg was always willing to give his time.

In August 1995, Stieg and a few others founded *Expo* magazine, a publication with the aim of defending democracy against extremism, organized racism and anti-Semitism, thus mapping organized racism in order to provide mass media and the public with the information they needed. This also meant that political discussions were not held in the office, since with time *Expo* would have co-workers with sympathies along the entire democratic political scale. They were mostly young people who, in the early days, would put in countless late-night hours without pay. The violent strategies of the extreme left were not their cup of tea, and this led some people to label *Expo* a "bourgeois" publication. The extreme right would call it a communist paper, of course, pointing to Stieg's leftist background as proof.

When *Expo* magazine first appeared on the market, it attracted the attention of democratic forces and of those at the opposite end of the scale. Its accuracy seemed to scare the extreme right, which by now was used to having a certain political initiative. The reaction did not take long in coming. Newsstands selling *Expo* had their windows smashed, with the warning that things would go from bad to worse if the owners continued to sell the magazine. The printer got the same message. The result was that *Expo* rapidly disappeared from the newsstands, without anyone really reacting at first.

Then suddenly the situation changed. Sweden's major daily papers finally realized that terrorism was about to suffocate a small – but brave – magazine and offered to help. A couple of papers actually gave space on their pages to publish *Expo*'s articles. This became known as "the *Expo* affair" and not only saved *Expo*, but also gave the magazine a great deal of publicity. At the time *Expo* issues largely consisted of detailed accounts of recent racist incidents, but Stieg and others soon shifted the focus of their articles to analysis.

Steig did not keep a low profile for reasons of safety alone. He preferred to work rather than to be seen, and he refused to be called editor-in-chief. The idea was to take a step back in order for others to learn how to run the place. If radio or television wanted to interview someone from *Expo* he would hardly ever go, but rather send somebody else instead.

In 2001 *Expo* became a national focal point for the E.U.M.C. (European Monitoring Centre on Racism and Xenophobia), and the most immediate effect of this was being invited to the governmental delegation at the U.N. Conference Against Racism, which was held in Durban in the days just before 9/11. Everybody expected that Stieg would be *Expo*'s man at the scene, but he refused. In the end I went, but I still think it a pity that Stieg did not go. He went to certain other places, however, among them New Scotland Yard in London, where he gave a lecture.

It was also in 2001 that a radical fraction group left the S.D., the major party on the extreme right, and founded the N.D. (the National Democrats). Gathering information about the split was of great importance to *Expo*, and it made us do something that at the time was rather unusual: we called the leading figures in both parties on the telephone, as we felt that this was a time when the rivalling factions might talk to us. And they did, at some length. But then the N.D. made a decision to cut us off from further contact. We were left with one choice: to plant one of our own members into the new organization as an undercover agent. Our chosen man was Daniel Poohl, who later became editor-in-chief at *Expo*. Daniel was soon absorbed by the N.D. and given the task by them of videoing all their activities. This undercover work went on for a number of weeks and included a journey with N.D.'s leading members to the Czech Republic, where secret meetings were held with various extreme-right organizations. Daniel's work for the N.D. was later exposed, but by then he had gathered enough material for a long documentary on one of Sweden's major T.V. channels.

In the early years the *Expo* editorial office would move between different places, always trying to keep its whereabouts a secret. But wherever the office would be, it would inevitably cost money, and this combined with the printing costs meant the financial difficulties eventually became so desperate that it looked as if the publication would have to be shut down, even though Stieg had more than once put in his own money to keep it afloat.

It was at this time that Kurdo Baksi approached *Expo*, declaring that he was prepared to have it published together with his own *Svartvitt* (Black and White) a magazine that focused on issues of integration. *Expo* accepted the offer and it proved to be a fruitful cooperation, even after *Expo* had gathered enough strength to stand on its own legs again.

As more co-workers were joining *Expo*, the premises felt small again. Then the business in the office next door closed down and Stieg suggested that we should rent that space as well as the old premises. We were still very short of money and the rest of us were not convinced by the idea. But one day Stieg just acted on his own and the expanded office was a *fait accompli*. Not only did it give us enough space to work there and receive people at the office, is also meant that we did not have to literally sit on our archives. Now they became much more accessible.

The archives assembled by *Expo* about organized racism were quite substantial even at the beginning, and they would grow. Stieg would take a great deal of pride in it and call it "the Heart of *Expo*", which was very much the point. There were – and still are – no other archives of this kind to be found in Sweden. Together with the research, they of course serve as the basis for the information given out to the public and the media. The archives eventually became so rich and extensive that they were copied by the Swedish Royal Library.

Stieg did not work ordinary office hours. He would usually come in after lunch, well into the afternoon, with an evening paper stuck under his arm. After summing up the day he would retreat to the adjoining room, where smoking was allowed. He would light up a hand-rolled cigarette and put his feet on the table. With his laptop literally on his lap, he would then hammer away with a smile, as if every word he wrote gave him satisfaction.

He would continue to work in the office until after midnight, and then return home and work more. It is still not quite clear to those us of who worked at *Expo* when he wrote the *Millennium* books, but it would be a fair guess to say that a lot was done in those early-morning hours.

Sometimes Stieg would walk out on to the roof terrace to have a smoke. Even though I do not smoke myself, I would sometimes join him there. It became our opportunity to have a little chat beyond everyday matters. On these occasions we would sometimes talk about widening *Expo*'s scope. We talked about initiating a column where representatives from all democratic parties would be invited to focus on their vision for a future democratic society.

One afternoon in the spring of 2003, Stieg came up to the office as usual. I could tell he was pleased about something, and soon enough he turned to me and said:

"I'm working on my pension insurance, you know!"

I thought this was rather an odd statement to come from him, since financial planning was one thing this otherwise brilliant man did not know much about. But I was curious and asked him what he was up to, thinking that he had found some good deal with a bank or an insurance company.

"I'm writing a crime novel and I'm trying to get it sold," he told me.

I smiled and said something about that being interesting, but to myself I wondered if his mind was getting a little soft.

One afternoon a couple of weeks later he asked me if I remembered that book he had told me about. I said I did.

"I sold it for real money!" he said, not jubilant, but with that sort of quiet pleasure he had when a plan of his had worked out well.

In the summer of 2004, Stieg came with his partner, Eva, and her sister to visit us at our summer place in the archipelago. He had seemed eager to make that visit and he was in a good mood. I do not recall any conversation about his books, yet I felt that he knew that their publication was going to be a turning point in his life. What I remember, though, is waking up very early one morning and hearing little sounds from the verandah just outside our bedroom. Glancing behind the blinds I expected to see some animal roaming around in the Nordic early-morning light. Instead I discovered Stieg sitting out there, on a chair in his usual working position, smoking, his legs up on the table and a laptop on his knee, writing away as if nothing would give him more pleasure at three o'clock in the morning.

The very last time I saw Stieg was when I arranged a debate at a teachers' conference about a week before he died. I remember being slightly nervous that he would not show up on time. But of course he made it. He always did.

A few days later he called to ask me if I could help out with *Expo*'s coverage of a major neo-Nazi demonstration in the outskirts of Stockholm. Of course I would, I said. I felt flattered.

My mobile rang when I was in the middle of my work a couple of days after that. Somewhat irritated, I had a look at the display and decided to ignore it. But soon it rang again, and I had the distinct feeling that the matter was urgent. I answered it. It was one of my former colleges at *Expo* asking for Eva's number. He told me that Stieg had suffered a major heart attack at the editorial office. After I hung up I felt sure that Stieg was going to make it. He always did. The shock was shattering when I learned that he did not.

Jonas Sundberg was one of the founders of Expo *magazine in 1995. Between the years 2000 and 2003 he worked full-time at* Expo, *maintaining the magazine's schools project and initially handling its contacts with the E.U.M.C. He is also a schoolteacher and lecturer on educational matters.*

WORKING WITH STIEG LARSSON

Eva Gedin

.The other morning I read an interview with the New Zealand film director Jane Campion. At the end of the piece, for no obvious reason except perhaps that the journalist is Swedish, she exclaims: "Everybody's reading that trilogy which is making Sweden so famous, about the reporter and that young woman. I just love the pair of them! Thank God for a different sort of characters from the gang of sullen old miseries in crime novels from the 1950s!"

By now I have read so many reviews, articles, newspaper columns and reports about Stieg Larsson. His name and books are always cropping up, and I have been interviewed *endless* times, hundreds of them – but nevertheless I was so impressed, and proud, when his name appeared in that particular interview.

Just think that the man I met for the first time in March 2004, nearly six years ago – quite unassuming, dressed in jeans and a T-shirt, with lively eyes behind his glasses, an apparently friendly, nice, middle-aged Swedish man – that he would come to mean so much to me, to the publishing house, to my colleagues and to countless readers all over the world. To think that his wildest dreams would come true. For despite his somewhat reserved air, there was also a measure of natural self-assurance about him that suggested he had a premonition that his crime novels, which he had been writing for so many years, might possibly become something truly significant.

And to think that those dreams would cause such division among his nearest and dearest. And that he himself would not be alive to experience how far his dreams came true, when finally he demonstrated with his *Millennium* trilogy how to write a good crime novel, and that he would earn such vast amounts of money and become at last financially independent. It is such a pity; it is so remarkable. It is like a made-up story of the kind Stieg Larsson would have been able to write himself.

Stieg Larsson was the first crime-fiction author I worked with as an editor. I had been working mainly on literary books, some memoirs, some non-fiction and also poetry. My boss, Svante Weyler, who was publisher-in-chief of Norstedts at the time, thrust Stieg's manuscripts into my hand and said, "Here's something for you to take care of."

At first I was not at all sure. This was new ground. But it was fun. And a rewarding assignment. I had seldom met such a fully fledged author. And one I found instantly likeable. A clever and pleasant man in his prime.

The manuscripts came in two fat green files labelled *Men Who Hate Women I* and *Men Who Hate Women II*. In the covering letter, Stieg wrote, "X said that you would be interested in looking at my crime novels. Obviously, I have nothing against that.

"I'm sending you the first two books in the series. Book I is called *Men Who Hate Women* – which is also the theme of the novels. I've written a synopsis for the first three books, which are linked in the form of a trilogy. The main character is a king-size oddball compared with most characters in Swedish crime novels. I can no doubt expand the series with as many more books as you would like. Part three will be ready by the summer."

Obviously, the very first contact we had with Stieg Larsson involved this marvellous mixture of humility and self-assurance.

The covering letter also revealed three important facts:

He regarded the first three books as a coherent trilogy.

The oddball was Lisbeth Salander, and indeed we had not met her like before.

Stieg Larsson's aim was to become a "real" crime novelist – we could expect a lot more books from him.

.

We read the texts and were immediately impressed. One of our readers was Lasse Bergström, the legendary publisher-in-chief at Norstedts, then already retired, who had published all sorts of writers from Sjöwall and Wahlöö to Ingmar Bergman. It was clear from his report that he had read all 1300 or so pages in scarcely five days. Looking back, it is astonishing that his judgment hit the nail on the head, and was such a good summary of our reactions when for the very first time we read anything by this crime-novel beginner:

"The author: a writer unknown to me. Editor-in-chief of *Expo*, just now in the news as publisher of a book on honour killings, rubbished in *Dagens Nyheter* in what seems to be a feminist civil war. [. . .] It is worth noting that I have never previously been able to read *two entire* novels by an unpublished writer one after the other. So even as he comes in through the door, Stieg Larsson can prove that he is any-thing but a one-off. [. . .] What is new about Stieg Larsson in relation to Sjöwall and Wahlöö, Mankell, Edwardson and other successful Swedes in a genre with rather too many practitioners is that he has a kind of encyclopaedic gift for literary tension and entertainment, and without any apparent effort can move between different planes of action with barely a noticeable change of gear. It is no coincidence that the two novels are long. Larsson is able to keep several plots going at the same time, and to bring all the threads together at the end. [. . .] But what distinguishes Larsson's two novels definitively from Swedish predecessors in the genre is not just their quick-change feats but above all his choice of principle characters. The dogged journalist Blomkvist no doubt has literary forebears, but I find it hard to think an equivalent of Lisbeth Salander anywhere else in the worlds of crime novels or films. [. . .] Larsson portrays her with both tenderness and humour, and against all the odds the way he does it becomes if not credible, then at least vigorous and absorbing."

Praise indeed from one of our leading publishers for over half a century and a man well read in crime fiction. He points out one more important thing: how Stieg succeeds in writing both imaginatively and logically at the same time, a rare and highly desirable combination – certainly one of the ingredients for success in a work destined to be a worldwide bestseller.

Stieg did not say much the first time we met. We invited him to a meeting at Norstedts, and Svante Weyler and I received him with great anticipation. We were also most curious to find out who this so-accomplished first novelist was. Stieg was relaxed, leaning back in his armchair as we waxed enthusiastic about how good we thought his manuscripts were and how we wanted to make a big publishing event of his books, and how remarkable we thought it was that he had delivered *two* complete books at the same time.

Stieg was from Norrland, and since I too had grown up in the north of Sweden I soon recognized the type. What could be understood as shyness was instead a typical Norrland taciturnity – northerners keep their counsel. They tend to sit on the fence. And he said, somewhat confidently, "I think of these books as my pension. If things turn out well I will scale down the work I do for *Expo* and spend more time writing." And his covering letter showed that he had it in him. This was a man who would be able to write many more books. He told us even at that first meeting that he was quite far advanced with the third volume, which he would be able to hand in within the next few months.

Stieg was pleased that we were so enthusiastic. Before the meeting we had decided to publish his books. We offered him a three-book contract – the first of its kind that we had ever written for an unpublished novelist – and the contract was for both the hardback and paperback editions – then highly unusual.

Soon after our meeting we sent him the contract for signature. We were keen to start the work without delay. It was a fantastic opportunity for us, to plan long-term – two complete manuscripts received, and a third almost finished.

You could say that Stieg set the tone of our collaboration in the first e-mail he sent after that meeting.

We knew nothing at all about the name or the person Stieg Larsson when we met him for the first time. But we did know about the work *Expo* did, tracking and keeping an eye on right-wing extremists and neo-Nazi movements. When I asked him about his C.V. his response was very sparse. He listed where he had worked and the non-fiction books he had written about the Extreme Right. I could not really work out what his job had been at T.T., the Central News Agency in Stockholm. Stieg said that it would be sufficient to say simply that he had worked at T.T. for twenty years, adding, "What else? I don't really know." Characteristically, when it came to his private life all he wrote was: "Partner. No children. Grew up in Norsjö and Umeå. Living in Stockholm since 1977."

No, Stieg never talked about his private life. In any case, we had not yet come that far in our relationship. He said nothing about whether anybody else had read his manuscripts; he didn't mention his family; he said nothing at all about the fact that a year or possibly a few years previously he had sent his first manuscript to the Stockholm publisher Piratförlag, one of Sweden's most commercially orientated houses with many bestselling crime novelists on their list.

I did not learn about those kinds of things until later. After Stieg was dead. When family and friends stepped forward and reported that Stieg had been talking about his crime novels for years, how he had been writing away and how several people had read his texts, and how, after the humiliating rejection from Piratförlag – who had not opened the packet containing his manuscript because they never accept submissions from unpublished writers – he did not, for whatever reason, get himself organized and submit them elsewhere. How in the end his colleagues stepped in and more or less forced him to send them in to Norstedts.

We had Stieg's full confidence from the start; there was no fuss about anything at all, but it was also clear what a hair-raising workload he had, and that his responsibilities at *Expo* must take first priority. He not infrequently boasted about how quickly he and *Expo* produced books. "You beat that if you can!" he joked.

So there was a very congenial atmosphere in all our dealings with Stieg. Not all authors are as straightforward to work with, but here was a man who often said, "Come on then, get that red pencil out!" He was a wholly unassuming person, and genuinely interested in hearing what we had to say. He was well aware, for example, that there were long-winded passages in the texts that needed to be abridged. Even in such cases he gave the impression of being a person sure of his own ability and the quality of what he had produced, and so he had no difficulty leaving us to get on with the work we were experienced at.

When I describe Stieg, I often worry that I am over-praising him, gilding the lily, but the fact is that there is no need to don any rose-tinted spectacles. Everything about Stieg was so special right from the beginning. He was what is called "a good egg", and that's all there is to it. Amusing and easygoing. More expressive and loquacious in e-mails than in the flesh. Frank and curious. Somebody you felt you could have a lot of fun with. He would say things like, "If only you knew what I know about that," or "That's a story I'll tell you one of these days, when we have more time."

In one e-mail, for instance, he talks about the background of a serial murderer, and the rape of Lisbeth Salander: "A rule of thumb has always been never to romanticize crimes or criminals, or to write in a stereotyped way about crime victims. In book one I base the serial murderer on a composite of three actual cases. Everything described in the book can be found in actual police investigations. The description

14

of the rape of Lisbeth Salander is based on a case that happened in [the upmarket quarter of] Östermalm three years ago. And so on."

Stieg often stressed that he hoped that I and the copy editor, Elin Sennero, would be harsh on his books. He appreciated editorial input, not least because he had often been on the other side of the process and knew how important it was for his text to be put through the mangle to make it as good as possible. For instance, I suggested a certain restructuring of the beginning of the first book, and he thought right away that it was a good idea. We discussed the characters and certain expressions in the dialogues, especially the way Lisbeth Salander spoke, her weight and her height, and quite a lot about Mikael Blomkvist's philandering.

But he also showed his more stubborn side when I pointed out that I did not think the title *Men Who Hate Women* was good. It sounded too hard. It could sound off-putting. It sounded more like a non-fiction title. Stieg promised to think about it. But he came back after a while and said he was certain that the first book had to be called *Men Who Hate Women*. We were welcome to change other things, but that was something he was not prepared to give way on. An instance of his more uncompromising side perhaps. As a publisher, one has to have a feeling for when it is appropriate to help an author to "kill his darlings", and when it is better to back off. Stieg's conviction about the title suggested it had a deeper significance for him, and I gave way. Apart from that, I have to say that Stieg turned out to be just as unassuming as he appeared, and that there were not very many "darlings" to kill off. It was all very positive, and the editing went smoothly in a very pleasant atmosphere. On both sides. The only discordant note was Stieg's incredibly high work rate.

Stieg's chief enemy was time – in more ways than the obvious one, we were soon to discover. Now he was reading the proofs of a paper that was to be published in connection with an exhibition, then he was due to give a lecture in Brussels, then he would be doing this and that and the other. But he would also book a week for revisions and checking the proofs. When he got round to it.

When I asked Stieg how on earth he had managed to write three long thrillers when he always had so much to do, he told me, "I don't need all that much sleep." It also became clear that writing his crime novels was his relaxation. He did it for the fun of it. And he obviously had so much fun when he was writing that he did not even bother all that much about submitting them to a publisher. That indicates plenty of self-confidence.

He was also curious about what we did in a publishing house. He wanted to know everything about our work. Did we edit on-screen or on hard copy? How many printed pages came from X manuscript pages? What format would the books have? How did we go about commissioning the covers?

When Stieg had completed the text of the third book after the summer of 2004, I wrote in an e-mail that it was such a pleasure to read it. It was perfectly clear by now that we had the privilege of working with an author with gold in his pen. Lasse Bergström wrote in his report: "I've spent the last three days or so in bed, reading Stieg L. 3 and only getting up to prepare the odd meal or to watch live football on the television. 'Unputdownable', as my old English scout used to say when he had found a commercially viable novel that also satisfied his demand for plausibility, excitement, thrilling depictions of people and settings etc. Very few, if any, English-language crime novels in recent years have induced me to stay in bed. But Stieg L. has achieved that with his almost unbelievable ability to keep track of high drama in the crime-novel genre – he has done it again, if anything even better than before. Book one was roughly speaking an orthodox crime novel with a self-contained mystery. Number two was a police thriller. Number three is a political thriller [. . .] But all three are closely interwoven, both as a depiction of a gallery of characters but above all as a much more provocative – and shattering – revelation of corrupt legal practices in Swedish society [. . .]"

In my e-mail to Stieg I quoted from Lasse's report, and Stieg replied,

"Great that you like number three. [. . .] It is most satisfying to see that Lasse noticed that I changed the genre from one novel to the next: he cottoned on exactly to what I was trying to do."

As always with Stieg Larsson, this balancing act between self-assurance and modesty. But Stieg was well aware that our enthusiasm for his books had communicated itself to everybody at Norstedts. More and more staff wanted to come and greet him whenever he came to visit, and more and more became involved in the preparations for the launch of the first volume of what we planned to call "The *Millennium* Series". He was really pleased about that. He many times stressed how much faith he had in us. "You are a big publishing house, I trust you – you run the show and I do the writing." Then one day, Stieg announced through clenched teeth, "All that book-signing lark and television chat shows . . . that's not for me." Stieg wanted his books to sell and was looking forward to the success – but anything to do with publicity and the media was something he hoped, by hook or by crook, to be able to skip. Hmm, I thought, that is something we will have to discuss. A successful book launch nowadays demands some input from the author. He'll get used to it. And maybe even get to like it. As things turned out, we shall never know. But he would probably have enjoyed the opportunity of talking about his books.

Stieg gave just one interview in his role as first-time author of crime novels, for the *Svensk Bokhandel* (the Swedish book-trade journal). Lasse Winkler, the editor-in-chief, knew Stieg, and thought it would be amusing to write about a former colleague who was going to publish his first work of fiction. (Eerily enough, the title of the article was: "A man for the history books".) In it Stieg mentioned several essential things about how he thought of his books and his new life as a crime writer:

"I started writing in 2001. I wrote them for fun. It was an old idea I had had from the 1990s.

"I reread Pippi Longstocking.* What would she be like nowadays? What would she be like as an adult? What would she be called? A sociopath? Somebody suffering from Attention Deficit/Hyperactivity Disorder? She has a different view of society from everybody else. I made her like Lisbeth Salander, twenty-five years old with a ginormous exclusion complex. She knows nobody and has no social skills whatsoever.

"Then you need somebody to counterbalance her. That was Mikael 'Kalle' Blomkvist,† a forty-five-year-old journalist. A know-all who works on his own magazine, called *Millennium*.

"There are lots of characters involved, a wide range of personalities. I work with three distinct groups. One group is based at the *Millennium* magazine, which has six members of staff. Secondary characters don't just drop in and say something, they do things in ways which affect the plot. It's not a closed universe. Then there is the circle around Milton Security, a private security company run by a Croat. And then there are the police, who have individual roles to play.

"It is only in the third volume that all the threads come together and you understand what has been happening. Each volume is complete in itself, but there is also something else going on. In your usual crime novel you never see the consequences of what happened in one story in the next book. But you do in mine."

Something which also emerges clearly in the interview is Stieg's knowledge of the crime-novel genre, and how consciously he has worked with it:

"I have been reading crime novels all my life. At T.T. I used to write two columns every year, in the summer and at Christmas. I picked out the five best crime novels recently published. The ones I chose included Sara Paretsky, Val McDermid, Elizabeth George, Minette Walters. Funnily enough, the crime writers I recommended were nearly all women. I know what irritates me in many crime novels: they

---

* The highly unusual heroine, as every Swede knows, of a series of novels by Astrid Lindgren.
† Kalle Blomkvist is Astrid Lindgren's child-detective hero.

are often about just one or two people but say nothing at all about the social context.

"I write extremely quickly. It is easy to write crime novels. It is harder to write an article of a thousand words or less when every single detail has to be 100 per cent correct. We are never allowed to make a mistake [in *Expo*] – if we do, we are condemned and attacked in the right-wing press.

"Writing crime novels means writing entertainment. It is not primarily a matter of making propaganda or literary classics. I mean, crime novels are one of the most popular forms of entertainment we have. And then if you try to have something to say . . . And I do have, of course."

He was secure in his new role: that is clear from the interview, and he knew the genre inside out. It was a matter of entertaining your readers – but if you had something to say . . . And he, of course, did have. When I now read a collection of his articles for *Expo* and other journals, I recognize Stieg's style, his unique voice. It is seriously committed, widely read and knowledgeable, and often has a dash of refreshing irony. Two sides of the same coin: the distance between the impassioned journalist fighting for democracy, struggling against racism and for feminism on the one hand, and Stieg Larsson the crime novelist on the other, was not as wide as one might think.

In October 2004 we were preparing for the Frankfurt Book Fair. We told Stieg that we would love to have a synopsis of the first two volumes to see if we could stimulate interest among foreign publishing houses. We had not expected to sell anything until after the first book had been published in Sweden – which was planned for the following autumn – but we thought we would take a few preparatory soundings, as it were.

It must have had something to do with the enthusiasm and commitment generated in those of us at Norstedts who had read Stieg's manuscripts, but the fact is that there was a buzz in Frankfurt around this unknown Swedish writer, and the German publisher Heyne made us a substantial bid for all three books. Our somewhat excited foreign-rights director, Magdalena Hedlund, had the honour of telephoning Stieg from the fair and informing him that the first sale had already been achieved, and that there was great interest among several of our Scandinavian colleagues.

Stieg was pleased, of course. And he knew his stuff. Of course. He knew that the German publishing house Heyne that had bought the rights was a part of the Bertelsmann/Random House group. R.H. was the American company that published many of the American crime novelists Stieg so much admired.

Now everything shot ahead at high speed. Swedish film companies had also heard rumours and expressed great interest. A preliminary meeting was arranged: Stieg was there, but still had faith in our ability to take care of "the business side". Everybody who expressed an interest was supposed to be included in negotiations.

Everything went to plan. Everybody was happy. We discussed our first celebratory party: a dinner with Stieg and his colleague who had been kind enough to recommend Norstedts. All that remained was to find a date that fitted Stieg's hectic timetable. We already had a lot of things to raise our glasses to. And we longed to sit down and talk and get to know our new writing star.

Late in the evening of November 9 I was telephoned at home. It was Svante, my boss, who said, "Eva, I'm afraid I have some bad news for you." Thoughts raced through my head. He sounded serious. "Stieg is dead." My mind went blank. How was that possible? What had happened? Could it be true?

The following morning all the staff at Norstedts assembled, the mood heavy with sadness and gloom. I still have a scrap of paper on which I scribbled down notes from a conversation with one of Stieg's colleagues on *Expo*: "Looked tired. Chest pains. Ambulance came pronto. St Göran, same block. Heart attack. Died 18.30. Funeral? Where? Help! Civil ceremony. Eva's sister helping with practicalities. Death notice. Eva, Erland, brother Joakim. Work colleagues including

Norstedts. Big international anti-Fascist network. England/Germany. Big burial ceremony."

It said in the obituary written by Stieg's colleague: "Stieg's work schedule was generally regular in its irregularity. He always arrived at the *Expo* offices around two in the afternoon, had 'forgotten' to have breakfast and lunch, and was forever juggling dozens of balls at one time. And then he would go on working until five in the morning.

"He found it difficult to say no to anybody who approached him for ideas or advice, to give a lecture, co-author a text and so on. And he helped everybody he could, with never a thought for himself."

The obituary also said that Stieg had just completed a trilogy of crime stories, which would be published by Norstedts the following autumn. We had no doubt that we would publish the books, even though Stieg was no longer with us. He had done his part. Now it was up to us to complete the job. And we were clear about one thing: the world and the characters he had created would live on.

During the years that have passed since we published Stieg's books about Blomkvist and Salander, I have missed him over and over again. It was quite a challenge at first, launching a crime-novel trilogy when its author was no longer alive. But we had total faith in the project. And we owed it to Stieg, to tell the world what he stood for and what he had created. But as Stieg's publisher it has felt empty and strange not to be able to pick up the telephone or write an e-mail and tell him about the latest developments. To be a sort of inferior stand-in when it came to interviews and discussions of the books.

There have been mutterings to the effect that some of the success has been due to the myth that has come into being, precisely because of Stieg's dying when he did. That is rubbish. The books have the strength to enable them to live on even if their creator is no longer with us. It is especially difficult nowadays when so much interest revolves around the author, and it is expected that the author is present to explain, and to say what and how he thought. That is a gap it has been impossible to fill. And it would have been a thousand times happier to share it all with Stieg. And a thousand times better if only I had had the opportunity of getting to know him properly. And it would have been a thousand times better to have had an author around to write a lot more books about Blomkvist and Salander.

Before publication day of the third and final book, we wondered if we had any more material about the books to present to the ever-increasing number of readers of the *Millennium* trilogy. I thought about Stieg's e-mails. Might there be something there? It was now the beginning of 2007, and just over two years had passed since Stieg died. I realized that I had not looked at our e-mail correspondence one single time during those years. It felt a little strange and unnerving to open it up on the computer.

But there he was again. His voice, his cheerful exclamations and our mutual joy in connection with this project which we never managed properly to share, but which so many other people have partaken of. Many more than we had ever dared to imagine. Such happiness and such sorrow at the same time. And then the feeling of pride. Such as when I received pictures from Swedes who had seen the advertising campaign in the Paris metro, or when *The Girl with the Dragon Tattoo* became number one in the *New York Times* bestseller list, or when Mario Vargas Llosa wrote a lyrical tribute to Stieg's heroes in a full-page article in *El País*. Such as when publishing colleagues from all over the world come to me and want to talk about Stieg's books, even colleagues who do not have the privilege of being able to publish them themselves. Such as when Jane Campion mentions Stieg in an interview.

Translated by Laurie Thompson

Eva Gedin was the first editor of Stieg Larsson and has since 2005 been Publisher of the fiction department at Norstedts Förlag.

The e-mail exchange between Stieg Larsson and his original publisher at Norstedts, Svante Weyler, his editor, Eva Gedin, and his line editor, Elin Sennero

Wednesday, 28.04.04, 18.10
From Stieg Larsson

Hi Svante & Eva,

The contracts arrived today. I will read them carefully, but I have the impression that you two are good people, and Norstedts is a publishing house to be taken seriously, so I do not need to worry about formalities.

As I said, I am pinned down more or less 24/7 until about 15 May when both the book and the magazine are due to go to press; so no matter how much I would prefer to devote myself to the crime novels, I am so committed just now that I hardly know whether I'm coming or going. Things should be much calmer after 15 May.

A few points:

*   Question: how many book pages are a million key strokes? Do you have a format template, or an upper limit for how long

your books can be? Book I is 360 MS pages; book II is 400 pages; book III looks like being 410–415 pages.

* Question: there are some 40 pages or so of book III still to write. I expect to be finished by the end of May/beginning of June. That will be the version in which the whole plot is in place, but I will need to polish the dialogue and spruce up details. That will take a bit more time. (Let's face it, we have plenty of time left before it needs to be put to bed.) However, my question is if you, Eva, would like to attack the MS with your red pencil at this stage and for me to do the rewriting after you've made your input, or whether you would prefer me to finish polishing the text before you start carving it up. In the latter case I reckon I will have finished checking all the details and so on during the summer, and you could begin your butchery around July/August.

* Eva: one more thing. How are we going to go about this in practice? You will no doubt want to chop and change the text. Do you want to edit it electronically, or would you rather work with a hard copy? Shall I send you the text as e-mail attachments?

* With regard to marketing book III, I have an idea which I've been toying with for a year or so. I would like to set up a home page (for the magazine *Millennium*). My question is: should I consult your marketing people in connection with this, or should I go ahead and cobble it together myself, or what? In other words, would Norstedts want to be involved in this home page?

* Some people who feature in the book need to be consulted. This applies first and foremost of course to Paolo Roberto, who plays a considerable part in book II. I have never met Paolo, but he works for Strix television nowadays, and both Robban and Mikael Ekman at *Expo* have already taken the piss out of him for needing to get help from a woman to be able to survive a fight. So he knows the score, and it should not be all that

difficult to talk him round. When I wrote him into the book, my thinking was that book I would already have appeared before I needed to chat him up; but then I'm afraid I scribbled away so rapidly that you received my MS before I had had a chance to talk to him.

Kurdo Baksi crops up in book III. Kurdo is my younger brother, and he'll just be thrilled to bits to be among the cast. But it is details like this that I need to sort out.

O.K. All the best,
Stieg

Thursday, 29.04.04, 15.06
From Eva Gedin

Dear Stieg,

Great to hear from you. And nice to hear that you think we're O.K. We think you are the tops as well!

I would expect your books (I have done the sums on the first two of them) to be 450–500 pages. It depends to some extent on the page layout and typeface we use. I think they should pack a punch. But not be too big. Just big. And attractive. And we will produce them in our big-novel format. I'll come up with examples to show you what all this means in due course.

I would prefer to read book III in its primitive form. Let's face it, it's fantastic to be able to have an overview of a whole series all at once. It makes it much easier to discuss the individual parts, and it means that consistency can be sorted out at a stroke, as it were, and avoid unnecessary duplication.

I have no intention of attacking any of the text with my red pencil yet. I thought it would be useful for us to meet and discuss the more significant changes we might need to make in book I. And you ought to meet your copy-editor, Elin, who is one of our best – luckily she will be able to get going on your text in the very near future.

I am thinking along these lines: your books are unusually well written, consistently. Most of the adjustments that need to be made are at "line-editing" level. Elin will do that, in consultation with me. So you will have an all-embracing discussion about your novels with me, and then a meticulous line-by-line going-through of the text with Elin. I can explain all this to you when we meet. (And you will meet Elin as well.) Generally speaking, we start by working on printed-out texts, and then we edit the electronic documents accordingly (but only if the author is prepared to let us have them – some authors insist on making all changes, major and minor, themselves, right through until the final version.) But you do not need to send me any electronic files at this stage.

I really like your idea of a home page. We can discuss this in more detail with our publicity manager and web expert. I also think that the series of books should have an overall title incorporating the word *Millennium*. But we can talk about that when we get round to discussing titles and covers.

I had intended to ask you about Paolo Roberto. If he is going to be in the series – and I think he can be, even if there could be problems when it comes to translations of the book (which I am confident can be resolved) – then we need to let Paolo R. read the text so that he knows exactly the context in which he's involved, and give his approval. Are there any more real persons mentioned in the novels, apart from the reference to Kurdo Baksi? I thought Paolo was the only one.

Anyway, I hope this has clarified a few things. I'm looking forward to sitting down and really getting to WORK on this fantastically exciting project. Sort out all the things you need to finish. We have plenty of time, and that is an enormous advantage when we're planning to launch these books in a really big way.

All the best,
Eva G.

Friday, 30.04.04, 21.44
From Stieg Larsson

Hi Eva,

I've just realized that it's Walpurgis Night. I had forgotten all about it. The young are muttering away and cannot wait to go home or go out for a few beers, and I've promised to let them loose after nine. Poor old Daniel Poohl – he's our assistant editor-in-chief and has been sleeping in the office for a couple of weeks now. They're going on about setting up a branch of the trade union. Hmm.

You'll get book III as soon as I've tied up a few loose ends.

I'm looking forward to meeting Elin. I am not altogether confident of my ability to put my thoughts into words: my texts are usually better after an editor has hacked away at them, and I am used to both editing and being edited. Which is to say that I am not oversensitive in such matters. Sometimes we will disagree about matters of fact, and like everybody else of course I have a few hobby horses I am unwilling to abandon. I think the first few chapters are a bit long-winded, and it's a while before the plot gets under way. The idea was really to build up a substantial gallery of characters and set the scene before the story got going. Etc.

I'm pleased to hear that you think the books are well written. That makes an old churner-out of texts feel happy.

You might be interested in a few of my thoughts concerning the books:

In many respects I have gone out of my way to avoid the usual approach adopted in crime novels. I have used some techniques that are normally outlawed – the presentation of Mikael Blomkvist, for instance, is based exclusively on the personal case study made by Lisbeth Salander.

I have tried to create main characters who are drastically different from the types who generally appear in crime novels. Mikael Blomkvist, for instance, doesn't have ulcers, or booze problems or an

28

anxiety complex. He doesn't listen to operas, nor does he have an oddball hobby such as making model aeroplanes. He doesn't have any real problems, and his main characteristic is that he acts like a stereotypical "slut", as he himself admits. I have also deliberately changed the sex roles: in many ways Blomkvist acts like a typical "bimbo", while Lisbeth Salander has stereotypical "male" characteristics and values.

A rule of thumb has been never to romanticize crime or criminals, nor to stereotype victims of crime. I base my serial murderer in book I on a composite of three authentic cases. Everything described in the book can be found in actual police investigations.

The description of the rape of Lisbeth Salander is based on an incident that actually took place in the Östermalm district of Stockholm three years ago. And so on.

I have tried to avoid making victims of crime anonymous people – so, for instance, I spend a lot of time introducing Dag Svensson and Mia Johansson before the murders take place.

I abhor crime novels in which the main character can behave however he or she pleases, or do things that normal people do not do without those actions having social consequences. If Mikael Blomkvist shoots somebody with a pistol, even in self-defence, he will end up in the dock.

Lisbeth Salander is the exception to this quite simply because she is a sociopath with psychopathic traits, and does not function like ordinary people. She does not have the same concepts of "right" and "wrong" as normal people, but she also has to face up to the consequences of that.

As you have probably realized, I have devoted an awful lot of space to secondary characters who, in several respects, play just as big a role as the main characters. The intention, of course, is to create a realistic universe around Blomkvist/Salander.

In book I Dragan Armansky was introduced in considerable detail: obviously he is going to be a secondary character who keeps cropping up. In book II the group of police officers around Bublanski and Sonja

Modig are given prominent roles. And in book III Annika Giannini and Erika Berger are much more prominent than in the earlier books. In book III another person appears who will be a regular member of the gallery of characters in future books. This is wholly intentional on my part. I think that secondary characters can often be much more exciting than the main player.

The only character with whom I have had difficulty is Christer Malm. In my original plot he was going to play more or less the same role as Erika Berger, but it didn't work with him as editor-in-chief. And so I was forced to invent Erika Berger, who became a much more entertaining character.

I am going to have a problem with Miriam Wu down the line – I don't really know what to do with her. The difficulty here of course is that Lisbeth Salander cannot acquire confidantes and at the same time remain an outsider. We shall have to see what happens.

As far as Paolo Roberto is concerned, I'll have a chat with him in the near future. Kurdo is not a problem. He's my "little brother", after all. We've known each other for many years.

All the best,
Stieg

Monday, 18.05.04, 09.15
From Eva Gedin

Hi Stieg,

I hope you have recovered after all that work you had to do in the first half of May. Will we be able to meet soon? Next week maybe? I can make Tuesday and Thursday p.m., or Wednesday a.m., or any time at all on Friday (week 22, that is).

Looking forward to getting the whole thing off the ground!

Greetings,
Eva

Tuesday, 25.05.04, 15.25
From Stieg Larsson

Hi Eva,

It's been a white-knuckle ride. In no more than thirty days we have produced a book from the concept to sending it to the printer, an issue of the magazine and a major investigation. We put the mag to bed at the weekend. Things should get much easier for me shortly, and remain low-key until September or thereabouts. It will be a bit hectic for a while yet – there are press releases to be sorted out, and I'm booked for meetings until the E.U. elections, besides having to catch up with routine stuff such as invoices and correspondence. But generally speaking I'll be free to start dealing with Norstedts again.

This week I'm fully booked on Tuesday and Wednesday, and I have to give a lecture in Malmö on Thursday. But Friday is fine. I'll be home by about noon, and can call in on you at about two if that suits. Then I'm at your beck and call.

Greetings,
Stieg

There is a break in the exchange during the summer of 2004

Wednesday, 11.08.04, 14.48
From Stieg Larsson

Hello Eva,

Here is book III, first draft.
   I'll finish polishing book I tonight and send it to you tomorrow.

   xxx,
   Stieg

One e-mail is missing here

Wednesday, 25.08.04, 16.30
From Stieg Larsson

Hi Eva,

Good Lord, it's never a good idea for editors to be under stress. But
I sent you Salander I two weeks ago, the day after I sent you book III.
   Have you received book III?
   And what I wrote in the covering letter was that I had made a few
small changes throughout the MS, but nothing major.

   Stieg

Thursday, 26.08.04, 09.00
From Eva Gedin

How odd. I received book III, and printed it out. But book I has only just turned up. All O.K. now.

Elin and I will be in touch once we've got under way with this. In other words, very soon. Our foreign-rights department, Magdalena Hedlund and Agneta Markås, will also be in touch as we shall start looking into foreign sales during the autumn.

I have promised to produce a detailed synopsis and notes on all the characters in book I and book II. If you have any contributions to make they would be most gratefully received. Obviously, you will be able to check the texts before we send them out, so you will have an opportunity to prevent us from putting about inaccurate rubbish.

And then there are the titles. I suppose I might have to give way on book I. "Men Who Hate Women"? I've been chewing that one over all summer . . . I'll try to come up with some alternatives, but I have the feeling you're going to get your way.

Best,
Eva

Thursday, 26.08.04, 15.10
From Stieg Larsson

Hello,

Great.

I have no idea what happened to book 1. It's two megabytes, which means that sending it via my I.P. swed.com can sometimes snarl up – but in that case I usually get an error message. I think.

In any case, you now have both books.

The synopsis is more or less illegible. It takes the form of hand-written notes in three different notebooks. I can make a clean copy if you like, but the plot has changed since the synopsis was written. For instance, Erika Berger does not feature in the synopsis: her role was played by Christer Malm, but he was so boring that I had to invent Erika.

I can send you the gallery of characters. I have added to it as I've gone along, although it's in several different places.

If you give way on the title for the first book I would be especially pleased and contented. I've also been thinking about it over the summer, but "Men Who Hate Women" is extremely good. I've asked a few friends what they think, and they all say it's a title that makes you look twice.

xxx,
Stieg

Friday, 27.08.04, 17.32
From Eva Gedin

Thank you, Stieg,

for the dramatis personae. It was extremely interesting and will be very useful. I'll give the go-ahead for visuals for the covers, so that the whole thing starts to become reality. And I have forbidden myself to start reading book III until I have finished book I. So it will be some time before I get back to you about that.

Rumours have already started spreading about your forthcoming launch as a novelist, and the series of books you are writing – the foreign-rights department is busy working out its strategies. It will be great, having that to make a song and dance about at the Frankfurt and Göteburg book fairs this autumn! There again I have the feeling we should tread carefully in these early stages. The books should be allowed to prove their own worth, if you see what I mean.

We can be in touch about this and that during the autumn.

How long do you think you will need to read our edited version of book I? Elin can no doubt let you have a timetable next week, so that you know when you can expect to find it in your letter box. But it would be good if you could read and approve it pretty quickly, as we want to be able to send out corrected proofs in the first or second week of October.

I hope things are less hectic for you now than they were in the early summer.

Best,
Eva

Monday, 30.08.04, 15.01
From Stieg Larsson

Hello Eva and Elin,

My agenda just now is that during September I am going to produce
an issue of *Expo* and, together with the reporter Daniel Poohl, write a
handbook on racism for Malmö museum. The book has to be written
and the layout completed by November 1 or so, and be ready for
distribution by November 30. Most of the work will be done in
September. (As you know we produce books within four to eight
weeks here at *Expo*; Norstedts ought to be ashamed of themselves.)
In addition I have five or six lectures booked, plus a lousy project that
we have to launch even so, and I also have to attend conferences in
Tel Aviv and Switzerland. No doubt there are a few other confounded
things to see to as well.

What are the dates of the Frankfurt Book Fair? When is the
deadline?

My suggestion is that I simply reserve a week at the end of
September/beginning of October when I can sit down and do nothing
but read Salander line by line, all in one go. Otherwise things will
get snarled up, I suspect.

Frankfurt and all that sounds great. Especially as you can decide
your own pace. I suspect you have more experience of that than I do.

Greetings,
Stieg

PS – Eva: I will probably have views regarding the cover visuals. I
usually hate or love covers, with very few shades of grey in between.
Let me put it like this: Guillou's covers for the Hamilton books are
definitely the kind of covers I dislike – all flat, figurative drawings, pop
art or naivism. Covers I like stir the imagination, are not all that easy
to interpret – possibly a detail of a larger picture. Sexist covers are

banned (and the definition of sexism is a matter of interpretation).

I don't remember if we ever talked about it, but I had an idea long before I came into contact with Norstedts that perhaps we could have an area of skin and part of a tattoo or a pierced eyebrow or something of that sort, as a recurrent theme. But over to you.

Tuesday, 31.08.04, 17.32
From Eva Gedin

Hmm, it was good to hear a bit about what you are involved in at the moment, you poor thing (?). But all will be O.K. if we can book you in to go through the MS that week you suggested. No problem from our point of view, everyone else will simply have to fit in.

But it is especially important now in the early stages that we are in agreement about changes that might have knock-on effects for future books. And it is also important that you consent to the cuts that we agree have to be made in Book I. In Book II there will not be nearly so many cuts, as far as I can see.

Thank you also for your thoughts about the covers. You are of course entitled to have views. We will no doubt develop several ideas which we can then weigh up, and pick out the best.

We've also been discussing Salander's weight, and think it ought to be about 42 kilos. At that weight you are decidedly on the slim side, but not unhealthily so. But I will carry on asking around. My method is simply to be rude and ask short, thin women how much they weigh.

We'll be in touch, enjoy your swimming.
Eva

Thursday, 2.09.04, 17.18
From Stieg Larsson

Hello Eva and Elin,

Thank you. Good. Several times I have been on the point of asking young girls on the Tunnelbana how much they weigh, but I resisted the temptation. It could be misunderstood, I reckon. But 42 kilos sounds about right.

I will avoid making a fuss about cuts.

I am aiming to be free in week 40, i.e. September 27 onwards, when I can clean up book 1.

Excuse me if I ask a question which might be very naive: if the Frankfurt Book Fair begins on October 6, won't it be difficult to have samples translated by then? Or how does it work?

Tatty-ta,
Stieg

Friday, 03.09.04, 14.17
From Eva Gedin

The way Frankfurt works, publishers who are keen to read extracts of the books they might be interested in have to be patient and wait until after the fair. We won't be finalizing any deals there in any case (that used to be the norm, but if it happens at all nowadays it is usually a put-up job to keep the old atmosphere and excitement going – we have e-mails and suchlike now). Obviously there is a lot of talk already. So it will not matter if we keep them in suspense until they get the MS.

But we have one bit of information to impart: no foreign agent or publisher is allowed to read your texts until October. So please do reserve that week for us – it would be terrific if that worked out. Elin and I are working at full stretch now. And enjoying it!

Have a nice weekend,
Eva

Friday, 03.09.04, 16.35
From Stieg Larsson

Hello,

What I have heard about the Frankfurt fair in the past suggests that it is like spending a few days in a little madhouse. I have no idea how selling foreign rights works, and have no intention of getting involved – but I assume it's about as exciting as holding an anti-Fascist congress for 120 groups of activists in Berlin, and trying to achieve some kind of ideological unity. But I think it is really great to hear that all of you at the publisher's seem to be so enthusiastic about the books, and think that they have the potential to be taken up abroad. I reckon that would make all of us happy and contented.

O.K., I'll set aside a few days in that week and deal with the MS of book 1 as a whole in one go.

Greetings,
Stieg

Friday, 10.09.04, 12.23
From Eva Gedin

Hi Stieg,

Elin and I are reading (and cutting) for all we're worth just now. And I can tell you that I'm enjoying myself no end. This is without doubt one of the most satisfying parts of my job. It's going to be great fun to discuss the details with you in due course.

We have also commissioned no fewer than three designers to work on the covers. As this is going to be a series that will keep on coming out year after year, we want to make sure it is right and really good from the very start. You will get to see what comes of this work a month or so from now.

I am also busy working on quite a long text for our foreign-rights department in which I describe you and the project, and I also include two synopses. Would you like to check these texts before we have them translated? Apart from that there is just one bit of information we would like from you for now: when did you start working for *Expo*? And you are certainly welcome to send us any other biographical facts you consider to be important. At the moment I know when you were born, where you live, that you were a features reporter with the Swedish Central News Agency (T.T.) for about twenty years, and that you are currently editor-in-chief at *Expo*. (And that you have published several non-fiction books, of course.)

Best wishes,
Eva

Friday, 10.08.04, 22.43
From Stieg Larsson

Hello,

Hmm, my biography . . .

I started researching right-wing extremism in the 1970s, and I suppose I have gone on doing that for more than thirty years. Since the early 1980s I have been the Sweden correspondent for the English journal *Searchlight*, which is the world's biggest and most prestigious anti-racist journal, and I was one of the founders of *Expo* in 1995. I have been working full-time for *Expo* since 1999. I have written books including *Extremhögern* [The Extreme Right] (with Anna-Lena Lodenius), which you could say was for a number of years the standard work on the subject; and *Sverigedemokraterna – den nationella rörelsen* [Sweden Democrats – the Nationalist Movement] (with Mikael Ekman), *Överleva deadline – handbok för mordhotade journalister* [Surviving the Deadlines – A Handbook for Threatened Journalists] (for the National Union of Journalists), and a lot of other weird things.

As far as T.T. is concerned, I was attached to several different editorial sections and had a variety of tasks. There is no such thing as a features reporter. To be pedantically correct, it should say that I "worked for T.T. Pictures and Features" for ten years or more. But perhaps it would be easier simply to say that I worked for T.T. for twenty years.

Anything else? I don't really know.

Greetings,
Stieg

Tuesday, 14.09.04, 21.56
From Stieg Larsson

Hello Eva,

I am attaching book II digitally as PDF files, so that all the typefaces are retained. I will deal with relevant maps and illustrations and so on later. If you would rather have the text in Word, I can fix that tomorrow.

I have been thinking a bit about the introduction and the tornado that devastated Grenada: the timing of last week's storm resulting in 35 deaths and the worst scale-5 tornado since 1954 was a bit unfortunate. I have been wondering about what to do with that section. In any case, we have resurrected the Grenada Committee here in Sweden as a result of the hurricane, so I will be able to consult the Consul. (I was involved in the revolution in Grenada in the 1980s, and was a good friend of the murdered Prime Minister Maurice Bishop. But that's another story.)

Living with a partner. No children. Grew up in Norsjö and Umeå. Living in Stockholm since 1977.

xxx
Stieg

Monday, 20.09.04
From Eva Gedin

Stieg,

I know that you and Elin are working flat out on the last bit of book I.

But a few other things.

Can you please send us the new version of book II? And please let us know what kind of changes you have made (so that I feel I am in control of what's going on!).

Could you please make the necessary corrections in the summary I wrote – i.e. the one we will be showing to foreign publishers. If I understood you correctly, you had a few things you wanted to change.

And – most important of all – could you get in touch with R. Aschberg* and check in your own diary to see when would be a suitable time to celebrate this fantastic project? Svante (and I) are available more or less all the time as long as you avoid weeks 45 and 47. If you can suggest a few possible times, I can book an appropriately lavish place.

Best,
Eva.

PS – And certainly we will shortly be looking at cover images. I will be in touch as soon as I have anything worth showing you. Soon.

---

* A well-known journalist and T.V. host in Sweden, an *Expo* board member and a friend of Stieg Larsson.

Wednesday, 20.10.04, 17.47
From Stieg Larsson

Hi Eva!

Sorry this is coming so late. I have been lecturing to the Office of the Prosecutor-General, and only just got back. I attach book II as a PDF file.

The changes I have made are peripheral, and there is nothing that affects the story significantly. It is mainly the occasional bit of dialogue or the wording of a sentence here and there, and other things like that.

The following things still need to be done before book II is ready:

* Paolo Roberto has to be consulted. I had thought of waiting until book I was published, but as things are now I suppose I must speed that up.
* Dag Svensson and Mia Johansson's home in Enskede needs to be made more specific. I have not decided yet which street it will be in, and I have to drive there and take a look at the neighbourhood to be sure that cars can take the routes they do, etc.
* A section in which Mikael phones Annika at the end will have to be recast so that it fits with book III.
* A passage involving Erika Berger needs to be reworded so that it corresponds with book III.
* A proper map needs to be inserted. The one there now has simply been downloaded from the Internet. I will make a real map myself so that we avoid problems with copyright etc.

I will play around with the summary. It is not strictly necessary, but I generally intervene when my editorial instincts start ringing alarm bells. And I think it is a good idea to start looking at book III as well.

I will come back to you about possible times for a party.

xxx,
Stieg

Thursday, 28.10.04, 17.21
From Eva Gedin

Hi Stieg,

I have now read the whole of book III – and it was such a pleasure! My God, but you are good! I am still as impressed as I was at the outset.

And here is a short report, or an immediate reaction if you prefer, from our reader who was the first one to read your work with great enthusiasm – Lasse Bergström, who was boss of this publishing house for many years.

"Hi! I've spent the last three days or so in bed, reading Stieg L. 3 and only getting up to prepare the odd meal or to watch live football on the telly. 'Unputdownable', as my old English scout used to say when he found a commercially viable novel that also satisfied his demand for plausibility, excitement, thrilling depictions of people and settings etc. Very few, if any, English-language crime novels in recent years have induced me to stay in bed. But Stieg L. has achieved that with his almost unbelievable ability to keep track of high drama in the crime-novel genre – he has done it again, if anything even better than before. Book one was roughly speaking an orthodox crime novel with a self-contained mystery. Number two was a police thriller. Number three is a political thriller, more like the Hamilton series than the two previous volumes. And Guillou can go and take a running jump! But all three are closely interwoven, both as a depiction of a gallery of characters but above all as a much more provocative – and shattering – revelation of corrupt legal practices in Swedish society, a concept not entirely unknown to a reader who spent his younger days as a journalist on the anarcho-syndicalist newspaper *Arbetaren*."

When you have the time, I would like to talk to you about the introduction, which I do think needs adjusting a bit. (That's the way it is – we publishers and editors always have to come up with a "but"...)

The covers are under discussion, but I have a visual I can show you to be going on with. It needs improving before it is good enough – but we're getting there.

All the best!
Eva

Thursday, 28.10.04, 23.39
From Stieg Larsson

Hi Eva,

Great that you like number three. It was a bit easier to write than the first two. Please tell Lasse Bergström that he is obviously an intelligent and sensible person of impeccable taste, and that flattery will get him everywhere.

Hmm. I cannot be sure, but I have the impression that you Norstedts people are seriously enthusiastic about my books. O.K., I know they are not bad, and of course I am delighted to read such flattering judgments: but I hope that you are not, for whatever reason, holding back negative comments. I am perfectly capable of coping with criticism.

It is most satisfying to see that Lasse noticed that I changed the genre from one novel to the next: he cottoned on exactly to what I was trying to do.

I have no doubt that the introduction needs adjusting. So, Madame Editor, let's hear what lies behind your "but".

xxx,
Stieg

The exchange ends here – Stieg Larsson died on 9 November, 2004.

Translated by Laurie Thompson

STIEG LARSSON:
THE UN-SWEDISH AUTHOR

John-Henri Holmberg

One afternoon in mid-April, 2004, Stieg telephoned me at the office.

Stieg was a friend of many years. We first met in the absurdly distant year of 1972, at the national Swedish science-fiction convention in Stockholm. Stieg, at seventeen, was a rather shy young fan attending his first convention while I, at twenty-two, was already a fannish dinosaur as I had cheated by starting out very early, publishing my first sf fanzine when I was thirteen.

When Stieg called that afternoon in 2004, more than thirty years into an ongoing friendship, it was to ask me to read and give an opinion on the contract he had just been offered by a major Swedish publishing house, Norstedts, which wanted to publish his first three crime novels.

That Stieg was writing novels was no great surprise; he always wrote and often spoke of his writing. When Stieg and his partner Eva Gabrielsson moved to Stockholm, the acquaintance that had begun in 1972 and continued for five years via letters and exchanges in the mimeographed fanzines we both published ripened into a close friendship when we lived in the same city, and that friendship lasted until Stieg's much-too-early death. We spent evenings together, partied together, worked together for three years on the board of the Scandinavian Science Fiction Society, where Stieg succeeded me as chairman. And we fought idiotic battles together when the idea to let female members have sole use of the club premises for one evening a week (since they made up a fairly small minority and since extremely boisterous and opinionated males otherwise dominated all discussions) turned out to be extremely controversial; the battle raged for a couple of years, and included such incidents as the time we arrived at the club to find the walls papered with hand-lettered posters featuring slogans like: "The S.S.F.S. Board of Directors: Worse Than Hitler".

Throughout all of this, being with Stieg was above all fun. He was a quiet man of strong convictions and with a great sense of humour. Or perhaps a strong conviction in the singular is enough; his most essential aspect was the uncompromising belief in every individual's right to liberty.

At a fairly young age, this lead Stieg to first become involved in the Swedish protest movement against the Vietnam War, then to become a Trotskyite, later to dedicate himself to the cause of combating everything he viewed as intolerance, repression or abuse. He fought racism, sexism, and imperialism. To Stieg, a fundamental conviction was defining; it meant that no compromise was possible. Probably his most basic tenet was the self-evident idea that all human beings are equally human, regardless of the colour of their skin, their gender, their sexual preferences, their religious or non-religious convictions or their other personal preferences. Stieg refused to associate with anyone he had cause to believe was intolerant, racist, sexist. Males believing themselves superior to women, whites believing themselves superior to non-whites (or vice versa), religious people believing that their religion gave them the right to denigrate others – these were the people Stieg would refuse to excuse, condone, or indeed have anything to do with. There were occasions when he discovered that friends of many years had abused a girlfriend, expressed anti-Semitic sentiments, shown themselves to be homophobic. From the day Stieg learned of these things, those people were no longer his friends. On that moral stand, he would never compromise.

This may all sound extremely serious. But again, Stieg was at bottom a quiet, humorous and friendly person. And a great smoker, a great drinker of black coffee and whisky. For many years, while working evenings and nights at the news agency where he was employed as a graphic artist, he would spend large parts of his days in coffee shops around Stockholm, reading, writing in longhand and talking to people he met or to friends who joined him for a while. He talked of writing the definitive guide to the coffee houses in the city, and could have done it. But instead he began writing novels.

Stieg Larsson was born on 15 August, 1954, in the small town of Skelleftehamn, with nowadays some 3,000 inhabitants. It lies by the sea around ten miles south of the larger Skellefteå city, now with a population of around 33,000, and some 500 miles north of Stockholm and around 150 miles south of the Arctic Circle. When Stieg was born, his parents were both in their teens and felt unable to take care of him; he grew up with his maternal grandparents on their Måggliden farm on the outskirts of the minuscule Bjursele community with sixty or so inhabitants, while his parents moved to Stockholm to find work. In 1962, when Stieg was eight, his grandfather died and Stieg along with his grandmother moved in with his parents, who had by now returned north with their second son, Joakim, who was three years younger than Stieg. The family lived in the larger university city of Umeå, a further eighty miles north of Skellefteå. In 1968 Stieg joined the countrywide anti-Vietnam War protest organization, where at eighteen he met fellow student Eva Gabrielsson, who became his life partner. By that time – and in fact since the age of sixteen – he was living in his own apartment

Stieg was an avid reader from an early age, and more uncommonly – particularly so in Sweden, where very few works in the field had been published at the time – he was a science-fiction enthusiast. He read the Swedish monthly sf magazine *Häpna!* – which was launched in 1954 and which folded in 1965 – and in its back issues became enthralled by Isaac Asimov's Foundation series; later, Robert A. Heinlein became a favourite of Stieg's early teens, but soon he began reading in English and found newer authors: Joe Haldeman, Frederik Pohl, Robert Silverberg, Samuel R. Delany, Joan D. Vinge, Stanislaw Lem, the Strugatsky brothers. At twelve he was given a typewriter and in his early teens he began trying to write science-fiction stories, first submitting a few to the semi-professional *Jules Verne-magasinet* (published from 1969 through 1971 with a total of ten issues by journalist and enthusiast Bertil Falk in Malmö), which were never published, later printing a handful in the mimeographed fanzine *Sfären* which he and another Umeå sf fan, Rune Forsgren, published from 1972 through 1974. During this time Stieg also tried writing novels, but, at least as far as I ever heard, finished only one of them, which he himself considered awful. Later, his writing turned to other subjects; by the time *Sfären* folded, he and Rune Forsgren had started another mimeographed fanzine, *Fijagh!*, where the emphasis lay not on amateur fiction but on essays, humour and political discussion. This last was hardly surprising. In Umeå Stieg had also become active in the Trotskyite Communist Workers' League and wrote regularly for their magazine *Internationalen*.

Why the very small Trotskyite group? Stieg Larsson was an individualist. His family background was more traditionally leftist. His maternal grandfather, with whom Stieg grew up, was an old-school Communist devoted to the Soviet Union, while Stieg's parents belonged to the ruling Social Democrat party in Sweden. Stieg rejected both these alternatives – he viewed the U.S.S.R. as a repressive totalitarian dictatorship and the Social Democrats as unprincipled and closely allied with capitalist interests. The Trotskyites, perhaps the most romantically utopian of any of the communist groups, were less intolerant in their cultural views than others, which generally viewed only socialist realism as acceptable and heaped scorn on both science fiction and crime fiction. They also, as had Trotsky himself, stood by the dream of an egalitarian anarchist and borderless world as the final goal, and this certainly spoke to Stieg's own individualism as well as imagination. During his military service at the infantry regiment in Umeå, in 1975 and 1976, Stieg was one of those smuggling the underground Trotskyite magazine *Röd Soldat* [Red Soldier] into the barracks.

But at the same time, Stieg was tolerant of other people's views and could even regard his own choice of affiliation with humour. Politics was, not surprisingly, a constant part of our discussions; most people who knew us both regarded our convictions as diametrically opposed, since Stieg was a card-carrying Trotskyite, and I an individualist libertarian. But in fact we often agreed on surprisingly many points. The bottom line, I suspect, was that we both felt that every individual had an inalienable right to life and liberty; the problem was just to decide which social system could best secure that right. I do know that the instant at which I knew that Stieg would be a friend for life was when quite early in our acquaintance I asked him if he could define, very simply, what he felt made his particular political group different from all the then many other communist groups. "I think the big difference," he said, "is that when all the others are out fighting you right-wingers in the streets, we are the ones who will still be sitting in our basement, trying to decide whether this is really the right historical moment."

1977 was a dramatic year. Stieg spent a part of it in Eritrea, where he had contacts in the Marxist E.P.L.F. liberation movement and helped to train a company of women guerrillas in the use of grenade launchers. But he also contracted a kidney inflammation and was forced to leave the country. In the early autumn, Eva Gabrielsson moved to Stockholm to study architecture, and a few weeks later Stieg followed. He had hoped to be admitted to the School of Journalism, but his application was rejected and instead he found himself working first at the Swedish Post Office's central sorting station, until he found more interesting work at Tidningarnas Telegrambyrå (T.T.), the leading Swedish news agency, where he started working in 1979 and remained until 1999. Stieg was employed as a graphic artist, but from the middle 1980s he also wrote a large number of feature articles, often popularizing science or debunking pseudo-science – Stieg, a confirmed atheist and rationalist, hated the wave of superstition peddled as "new age spiritualism" – but not least about literature, where he did semi-annual overviews of new crime novels published in Sweden and interviewed writers at the annual Swedish book fair. His interest in crime fiction was almost as long-standing as his interest in science fiction, and he followed both fields keenly.

Simultaneously, he continued to write outside of his employment. From 1982, he was a Scandinavian correspondent for the British *Searchlight* foundation, and began the work of exposing racist and fascistic organizations which would occupy him for the rest of his life. In the late 1980s he left the Communist Workers' League, unwilling to defend undemocratic foreign socialist regimes. In 1991 he published a major work, written with Anna-Lena Lodenius, *Extremhögern* [The Extreme Right], a history and survey of right-wing extremism in Sweden. This was later followed by further non-fiction books about right-wing organizations as well as an anthology of essays on the debate on "honour"-related violence against women and by a short guidebook based on his own experiences: *Överleva deadline – handbok för mordhotade journalister* [Surviving the Deadlines: A Handbook for Threatened Journalists]. And in the early 1990s he was one of the founders of the Hill Foundation, in 1995 renamed the *Expo* Foundation, a Swedish organization similar to *Searchlight*; in 1995 he was also one of the two founding editors of *Expo* magazine, a quarterly which first failed but was revived in 1999 with Stieg as editor-in-chief, and is still published today.

Stieg's investigation of fascist-inspired Swedish organizations harks back to his early years as an active science-fiction fan, when one of the readers of his fanzines was a young sf reader in Malmö, Lars-Göran Hedengård, who in his letters of comment (the most common way in which fanzine readers "pay" for the publications they receive is by commenting in writing) expressed such dramatically opposing views that much of Stieg's writing in some issues was devoted to arguing with Hedengård. It gradually became clear that Hedengård was active in several right-wing organizations, including not only Demokratisk Allians [Democratic Alliance], which supported the American military involvement in Vietnam, and the Svensk–Chilenska Sällskapet [Swedish–Chilean Society], which supported Pinochet's military government in Chile, but also Sveriges Nationella Förbund, S.N.F. [Swedish Nationalist Association], founded in 1915 and originally a royalistic, nationalistic and conservative youth organization which during the 1930s developed into an openly pro-Nazi party with its own uniformed guard corps. When S.N.F. split in the 1980s, Hedengård in fact became one of the leaders of its Malmö splinter group, which in 1990 applied for membership in the American Ku Klux Klan and in 1991 became the Swedish section of the international N.S.D.A.P.–A.O. [National Socialist German Worker's Party – Foreign Organization], which claims to be the official continuation of Hitler's party in Germany.

Even earlier, Stieg had learned that in Umeå, then considered the most politically radical city in Sweden, there was a small group belonging to the Nordiska Rikspartiet [Nordic National Party], at the time Sweden's most openly neo-Nazi political party. The additional fact that another science-fiction fan of about the same age was actually a member of an organization wanting to revive Nazism seemed not only ridiculous to Stieg – not least because the inevitability of change along with tolerance for even the most alien forms of intelligent life are probably the two most basic beliefs expressed in most science fiction – but also inspired his curiosity about both the existence of such organizations and what could attract people to them. And so he began the investigation, which would in the end become his career, of racist and fascist groups.

In the late '90s, Stieg was once more writing fiction. Initially short stories, to amuse himself and try his hand, often based on current news or on actual events that he had covered as a journalist. Then

59

something gelled. Stieg had wanted to write fiction since his early teens. And at forty-five, he realized that he knew what he wanted to write about. During the first years of the century, public debate in Sweden was largely preoccupied with "honour killings". The debate became explosive after the murder, in January 2002, of twenty-six-year-old Fadimeh Sahindal, who had left her Kurdish family after refusing to submit to their morality and became a public figure after giving a speech to the Swedish parliament about the plight of young women in many immigrant families. Fadimeh was killed by her father, who claimed that she had dishonoured her family by openly criticizing its traditional morality, and the subsequent debate mainly centred on the "honour" culture nourished by many recent immigrants from the Middle East. But at fifteen, Stieg had witnessed a rape when boys his own age violated a girl they all knew. Stieg did not participate, but neither did he try to prevent what happened. After a few days, he phoned the girl to ask her forgiveness. She told him that she never wanted to speak to him again. And he felt that she was right.

Two months before the murder of Fadimeh Sahindal, a twenty-two-year-old fashion model, Melissa Nordell, was murdered by her boyfriend, with whom she had tried to break up. Apart from the sensation stimulated by the victim's beauty and the brutality of the killing, this gave rise to no particular public debate; it was a "normal" Swedish killing, born of jealousy.

But to Stieg, this was taking the easy way out. He called the two women "sisters in death", and took the position that they had both fallen victim to the same male inclination to control women with violence.

He wrote about this repeatedly, not least in an essay in a book he edited in collaboration with journalist and anthropologist Cecilia Englund, called *Debatten om hedersmord* [The Honour Killing Debate], published in early 2004. But he also wanted to express his views in fiction, and he wanted to centre his story on a woman. Years earlier, in the early '90s, Stieg and his superior at the T.T. news agency, Kenneth Ahlborn, had been co-writing a feature on the classic juvenile detectives, those popular among young readers of the '50s, '60s, and '70s. In the only interview Stieg ever gave as a novelist, to Lasse Winkler, the editor of the Swedish book-trade journal *Svensk Bokhandel*, he said, "We were kidding around, talking about how you could write about those characters in their forties, facing one last mystery. That planted the seed, but nothing materialized back then." But in 2001, Stieg remembered that conversation, he said. "I considered Pippi Longstocking" – the famous character created by the Swedish children's author Astrid Lindgren, a pre-teen girl living alone in her own house, with a huge fortune, strong enough to lift a horse and impervious to the traditional morality of adults, teachers, police and society – "and wondered what she would be like today. What kind of an adult would she be? And what would people call a person like her? A sociopath? Hyperactive? Wrong. She simply sees society in a different light. I would make her twenty-five years old and an outcast. She has no friends and is deficient in social skills. That was my original thought."

So he had his idea for a main character, and a secondary one quickly followed: another Astrid Lindgren character, the boy detective Kalle Blomkvist, "only now he's forty-five years old and a journalist. An altruistic know-it-all who publishes a magazine called *Millennium*."

Melissa Nordell and Fadimeh Sahindal were both murdered. The public debate, in Stieg's view, aimed at stigmatizing violence against women by immigrants in order to cover up the hatred against women displayed by western males. This gave him the theme, and his intended overall title for the novels: "Men Who Hate Women". For according to his typescripts, that is the overall title for what he first planned as a series of five novels, and later extended to ten. The first book would have had the subtitle "*Millennium*", the second, "The Witch Who Dreamt of a Can of Petrol and Matches", the third, "The Exploding Castle in the Air". When eventually the books were published Stieg was dead and the titles had been changed. The series title became, not very aptly, *Millennium*. At least in Swedish Stieg's series title was kept as the subtitle for the first volume; in the English translation, it was thrown out altogether and the book was called

The Girl with the Dragon Tattoo. I suspect that he would have objected in no uncertain terms.

Stieg was a fast writer, but also a systematic one. He prepared an outline, as noted above, for five novels, later extended to cover ten. Then he started writing the books in his spare time, usually from sometime after midnight, when he had walked home from the *Expo* office, until the small hours of the morning. The manuscript of the first novel was finished sometime in early 2003 and sent off to Piratförlaget, a small Swedish publishing house known for its effective campaigns, its huge sales, and its strong crime-fiction list. Stieg kept writing the second book, while the first was returned by the post office – Piratförlaget had declined even to sign for the parcel. Eva went there to deliver the manuscript in person, since the house had promised to take a look at it, but after a few months a form rejection followed. By then the second book was almost done and the third was started. One of Stieg's friends, Robert Aschberg, read the manuscripts and offered to recommend them to his publisher, Norstedts. In April 2004, Norstedts offered Stieg the contract for the first three books that he asked me to take a look at before signing it. The rest, as they say, is history, though sadly in part hidden: according to the e-mail correspondence we had during the months before his death on November 9, the fourth novel was three-quarters finished, and the fifth well begun.

But what we do have are the three books he wrote, and when I had read them in manuscript, I told Stieg that they would make him rich. He said that he knew that; they were his pension. I said that he had no idea how rich; his were the first Swedish crime novels I had read which would outsell Maj Sjöwall and Per Wahlöö internationally. At that he laughed. Luckily, for once I can prove my prescience; it was quoted in the interview Stieg gave *Svensk Bokhandel*, printed a few days before Stieg's death, and later published also in the *Daily Telegraph* (4 June, 2010).

But why did Stieg's novels become the international phenomenon they are? My suggestion is that it is the result of several factors, and one of them, valid both within and outside of Sweden, is their relationship to Swedish crime fiction in general.

Reviewing Stieg's first novel in the third issue, 2005, of the Swedish quarterly *Jury*, a magazine devoted to discussion and analysis of crime fiction, I wrote in part that it was "not only an excellent first novel, but the best first Swedish crime novel I have ever read; a dense, finely plotted, intelligent and many-layered book towering almost embarrassingly above virtually all other Swedish thrillers and mystery novels. [. . .] Stieg Larsson for many years occupied a central position in Swedish public debate, as editor-in-chief of *Expo* and a leading expert on anti-immigrant and fascistic movements. And today's Swedish crime fiction is extremely sensitive to popular trends; most novels are about exactly those kinds of crimes currently most discussed in media and political debate. Consequently I suspect that many expect [Stieg Larsson's novel] to adhere to this norm and be about paedophilia or trafficking. It is not. Stieg devoted his working hours to debate and social issues; he wrote his novels in his spare time, and perhaps because of that he chose not to base them on the issues with which he dealt on a daily basis. In saying that, I have also said that his novel largely breaks with the current mould of Swedish crime fiction. You will find no defeated, lonely and middle-aged protagonist. You will find none of the typical pessimism and tired listlessness. You will not even find the otherwise obligatory nostalgia for the exploded Swedish ideal of the cradle to grave welfare state. [. . .] If we are to talk about traditions, this novel does not belong to the hardly challenging Swedish crime-fiction tradition, but instead to the far broader and from a literary standpoint more interesting Anglo-Saxon one."

To foreign readers, Swedish crime fiction is in most cases at best a handful of individual authors. The first Swedish crime writers to make an international impact were Maj Sjöwall and Per Wahlöö, who together wrote a series of ten police procedurals published between 1965 and 1975. Very much in the vein of the 87th Precinct series of novels written by the American author Evan Hunter under his Ed McBain pseudonym, some of which Sjöwall and Wahlöö translated into Swedish (although it should be mentioned that they denied having read McBain before starting to write their own series), the police collective headed by Martin Beck in the Sjöwall and Wahlöö series was a novelty in Swedish crime writing. The murders were brutal, the daily existence of the policemen gritty and ultimately defeating, the writing terse and journalistic and the books were explicitly political.

Before Sjöwall and Wahlöö, Swedish crime fiction was totally dominated by the puzzle-mystery tradition exemplified by authors like Agatha Christie and John Dickson Carr. From the '40s until the mid '60s, four authors dominated the field. First out was Stieg Trenter (1914–67), whose amateur sleuth, photographer Harry Friberg, in cooperation with police inspector Vesper Johnson solved well over twenty-five cases in as many novels published from 1943 onwards. Next came Maria Lang (the writing name of Dagmar Lange, 1914–91), whose many books were generally strong in romance but weak in plots. Third was Vic Sunesson (the pseudonym of Sune Lundquist, 1911–75), with policeman heroes solving mysteries in an idyllic, bourgeois Stockholm. Fourth and last was Hans-Krister Rönblom (1901–65), who from 1954 published ten cleverly plotted and slyly ironical novels, set for the most part in elegantly described small towns and featuring the mystery-solving historian Paul Kennet.

There were Swedish crime authors before the 1940s, but with the sole exception of expatriate Frank Heller (the pseudonym of Gunnar Särner, 1886–1947), whose humorous thrillers can be compared to those of the French author Maurice Leblanc, none of them have remained readable, if indeed they ever were. Instead, Swedish crime readers read translations, chosen almost exclusively from among traditional puzzle mysteries published in Britain, America and France. Conan Doyle, Dorothy Sayers, G. K. Chesterton, Agatha Christie,

John Dickson Carr, Ellery Queen, Rex Stout, Georges Simenon, later Chandler and Hammett: these were the most-read writers of crime fiction in Sweden.

Perhaps interestingly, they remained so long after having been superseded by new authors writing new kinds of crime literature in their own countries. Beginning around 1950, a number of Swedish publishers launched lines of monthly paperback originals, mainly translated and sold only through newsstands and tobacconists, not in traditional bookshops. Here the post-war crime writers were introduced to the Swedish reading public: this was where James Hadley Chase, Mickey Spillane, Donald Hamilton, John D. MacDonald, Ed McBain and many others were published in Swedish. Critics never dealt with these novels; if they mentioned them at all, it was to dismiss them as trash. Booksellers pretended that they did not exist, and, in fact, by not being sold through bookshops they were not considered to be books at all. Nevertheless they sold in huge numbers, and even if publishers who sold through bookshops alone kept publishing only "civilized" and "literary" crime writers, the hard-boiled and *noir* paperback originals made the reading public eager for new kinds of entertainment fiction also from Swedish writers. Sjöwall and Wahlöö, as suggested, made the great break with tradition: they abandoned the drawing-room puzzles, the single or at most paired hero, the gentlemanly criminal and the bloodless murders. And they were the first Swedish crime novelists to be translated globally.

Their popularity with readers, as well as with critics and publishers abroad, obviously called for emulation. However, Maj Sjöwall and Per Wahlöö were not content with writing their novels. In an essay published in 1966, the year after their first co-written novel, *Roseanna*, they stated their literary objective. Under the series title "Novel about a crime" they would write ten books, using the stylistic and thematic methodology of crime-fiction in order to reveal and analyse the hollow emptiness of the mixed-economy welfare state. Entertainment to them was a method, not an end; in each book, readers would be exposed to and forced to take a stand on ever larger and more fundamental factors at work in modern society. Crime, in these novels, was not an evil committed by individuals, but symptoms of a diseased social system, where the criminal just as much as those harmed by crime is a victim of socio-economic factors beyond their control.

In Sweden, the youth revolt of the late '60s and early '70s was not multi-faceted, as in most western countries, but uniformly socialist, and largely as a result cultural debate as well as fiction became politically radicalized. In this climate, Sjöwall and Wahlöö through their socialist ideals recruited a generation of new readers to crime fiction, and other authors followed their lead. For almost thirty years, the legacy of Sjöwall and Wahlöö – tired and depressed police collectives and socialist politics – dominated Swedish crime fiction, reaching their highest literary expression in the works of Henning Mankell.

Finally, in 1998, this general mould was broken. Liza Marklund introduced a journalist heroine and became immensely popular, as did Camilla Läckberg five years later with her series about amateur sleuth Erika Falk, and others. During the last few years, the number of original Swedish crime novels published annually has grown to over a hundred. But to a large extent a new but traditional mould has been added to the earlier one. Where the crime-novel protagonists used only to be policemen, beset by relationship problems, overwork, doubts and feelings of inadequacy, there are now also amateur detectives in novels where the depiction of their relationships, domestic problems and daily lives are often given at least as much space as the crime story itself. Perhaps the most basic trope of the Swedish crime novel throughout its existence has been the ordinariness of its protagonists. There have been no memorable Swedish eccentrics like Sherlock Holmes, Nero Wolfe or Hercule Poirot. Nor have there been any avenging private eyes like Mike Hammer, Travis McGee, V. I. Warshawski or Kate Mallory. Swedish twentieth-century literature, in fact, is peculiarly devoid of heroes, the "common man" instead being the preferred protagonist prototype.

This is one point where Stieg's novels make a dramatic break with Swedish tradition. Actually, it would be more strange if they did not.

Stieg's reading of choice was science fiction and crime fiction, both of which he read mainly in English, and neither of which was considered a respectable part of Swedish literature. And his reading language of choice was English. He once surprised me by stating that he preferred to read even Sjöwall and Wahlöö's novels in American paperback editions. "I just can't relate to crime novels in Swedish," he said. "If they are to sound real, they have to be in English." The first essay on crime fiction I have read by Stieg was written in 1975, when he was twenty or twenty-one, and deals with his three favourite crime writers, whom he characterizes as "If Hammett was the first, and Chandler the best, you can probably say that [Ross] MacDonald is the most interesting." He notes in passing that the "puzzle school has had a detrimental influence on the [Swedish crime-fiction] market". Later, when reviewing newer crime novels, he tended to appreciate mainly female authors; among those he praised are Val McDermid, Elizabeth George, Sara Paretsky, Carol O'Connell, and Minette Walters.

So what Stieg Larsson gave Swedish readers was novels written in the Anglo-American crime-fiction tradition, with the larger-than-life heroes and villains as well as the basically optimistic, action-oriented attitude of that tradition. In other words, to Swedish readers, Stieg's novels offered the kind of fiction they had earlier read only in translation, for the first time placed in familiar Swedish settings.

If Stieg's novels broke with the traditions of Swedish crime fiction, they also broke with the more fundamental traditions of Swedish attitudes and beliefs. This is more difficult to discuss, and perhaps must be approached in a slightly roundabout way.

In 1982, the German poet and essayist Hans Magnus Enzensberger wrote of the mill-town tradition in Sweden and of its influence on Swedish society:

"Lofsta mill is a wilderness enclave, a square plot of ground claimed for order, security and discipline. A high, yellow wall

67

separates it from the outer world, where lurk unpredictable animal forces. This wall is not only of symbolic importance, but also has a practical purpose: it protected society against wolves … Each one belonging there received from the mill not only on his own behalf, but on that of his family, employment and a place to live, schooling and spiritual guidance, medical care and old-age security for life, and even the voice of culture, i.e. that of the Niclas Cahman organ . . . was there for all. You have to be deaf and blind not to recognize the breeding ground of modern Swedish welfare society in this patriarchal utopia."

Enzensberger added that the mill town, with its owner's estate on a hill at one end, its graveyard at the opposite end, and its ordered rows of houses, church, school, infirmary and foundries still very much reflected the nature of modern Sweden. "Even the wall is still there, no longer physical but mental, no longer keeping the wolves out but the Swedes in."

What is important here, I believe, is that the roots of the Swedish welfare state lie deep in both history and tradition. Lofsta was founded in the seventeenth century, and when industrialism on a larger scale came to Sweden during the nineteenth century, it largely followed this model. Landowners imported German engineers to build and oversee factories, and to reschool the already extant farm workers into industrial workers. Whereas in other countries workers flocked from the countryside to the cities in order to sell their labour to industry – a situation which, on the one hand, created visible poverty in the cities which gradually led to political reform, but which, on the other, also transformed the previously landlocked peasantry into free agents and thus led to increased social mobility – in Sweden industrialism had little of this liberating effect. Swedish cities grew only slowly, and when the Social Democrats gained power in 1932 – since when they have ruled the country for sixty-five of the past seventy-eight years – it proved relatively easy in the long run for the party to identify itself with the social security system actually instigated long before in what Enzensberger called the "paternalistic utopia" of the mill town, which now on a larger scale became the model for Swedish society as a whole.

In the *Independent* (1 October, 2009), Nick Fraser wrote that: "Like any other society, Sweden has its own illusions . . . In Sweden, as elsewhere, the power of money has proved overwhelming. With their narcissistic sense of being the last progressives, intent on defending the cherished model of social equality, Swedes feel the change keenly . . . A second Swedish illusion is centred around the country's attachment to high-minded neutrality . . . The third and most important Swedish illusion is that the State is somehow moral, representing the views of its citizens." The same note is sounded in Ian MacDougall's review of the three *Millennium* novels (*n+1*, May 2010), where he writes, "The system has a hand in all aspects of Swedish life. If you can't trust the system, what can you trust? In the best Swedish crime novels . . . the cradle-to-grave welfare system takes care of its wards. But you start to wonder just which meaning of 'to take care of' that phrase refers to, and whether the all-too-visible hand of the state isn't rocking the cradle over an open grave."

This, I believe, is both apt and quite important when applied to the success of Stieg's novels. Probably the belief most cherished by Swedes is the idea that Sweden alone among the nations of the world has managed to find a righteous and just middle way between excessive state repression and the excesses of the market. This middle way is the welfare state, where a benevolent bureaucracy run by impartial and honest civil servants works tirelessly to ensure the well-being of all. When the occasional deviation from this is disclosed, it is normally considered an unhappy aberration but very seldom a sign of any systemic fault. An important part of this is that Swedes regard themselves as part of a society unique in its embracing of solidarity, a view which leads most Swedes to beliefs such as that Swedish health care is superior to that of any other country, and that women in Sweden enjoy a higher degree of equality than anywhere else.

These attitudes are common to most Swedes and to most Swedish fiction. But they are very much lacking in Stieg Larsson's novels. Despite being a Swede, he viewed Swedish society from the outside. In part, I suspect, this was due to the strong affinity he felt to his maternal grandfather, Severin Boström, who because of his Communist convictions during the Second World War was incarcerated in the concentration camp Storsien, where enemies of the Swedish state were put, and who for that reason was later largely an outcast in society. [It should be noted that Stieg Larsson's father claims that this story is untrue; since Stieg nevertheless believed it to be true, its possible falsehood can hardly matter. Stieg, for his part, published much of his radical political writing in Trotskyite publications under the pen name "Severin".] At the same time, it was probably also in part because of his early reading of science fiction, with its explicit message that change is the only constant, and that all we consider firm and unchangeable is in fact transient. Finally, it was probably also in some part due to his internationalism and early exposure to the Trotskyite critique of the state and dreams of a stateless society, which are certainly very different from the dominant Swedish views. In other words, when reading Stieg's novels, you are reading novels by an author weaned on American and British science fiction and crime fiction, who looks at Sweden without any inherent conviction of its moral superiority or unchangeability. And in his novels, one by one, he questions or explodes the basic tenets of the Swedish consensus.

The first novel – as do all three of them – intertwines two kinds of plots, one a financial thriller, the other a traditional puzzle mystery. In the financial thriller, a man who is not only a billionaire but also a hero of the purportedly egalitarian Swedish society is shown to be an immoral swindler and exploiter; in the puzzle mystery, he exposes the pro-Nazi currents in Sweden prevalent during the period up to and including the Second World War, and he also initiates the scalding exposé of hatred of and contempt for women by men of every social stratum, which is the major theme of the novels.

In the second novel, which combines what is essentially an espionage story with an action thriller, the illusion of Swedish moralistic neutrality is torpedoed by the story of how the Secret Service protects a brutal K.G.B. defector in order to sell his secrets to other countries, even to the extent of conspiring to cover up violent crimes and murder. The theme of men's hatred of women is continued, and here, as in the first novel, we meet men of all kinds and belonging to all social strata, from spies to policemen, from lawyers, psychiatrists and politicians to outlaw bikers, many of whom have in common a willingness to brutalize, use and silence women.

In the third novel, which combines a courtroom thriller with a police procedural and to some extent a lone avenger story, the state itself is shown to be morally bankrupt, and its officials and servants, from the prime minister down, to be all too willing to sacrifice the rights, welfare and even lives of individual citizens in order to hang on to their positions, privileges and power. Officials lie to, steal from, harass and murder the citizens they are supposed to protect and cherish. Even Henning Mankell, famed for his depiction of the gradual decay of the Swedish welfare system, retains a nostalgic longing for it; he and other left-wing critics of its current state repeatedly look back to the period from the '50s to the early '70s, when the vision was theoretically still fresh and no stain had yet marred the Swedish utopian dream. But what Stieg's novels show is that hypocrisy, not moral superiority, is the basis of the state, and in so saying he is the most un-Swedish of all Swedish authors. His criticism is systemic, not specific, and this sets him apart from not only other Swedish crime writers, but from most Swedes. In his novels, as in his personal convictions, the state is never fully moral or benevolent; it is always, even at best, also an instrument of violence, wielded against individuals who threaten the privileges and power of those who have managed to gain control of it. The "castle in the air" (a Swedish expression with the same connotations as the English "pipe dream") in the original title of the third novel, "The Exploding Castle in the Air", can hardly be interpreted as denoting anything but the welfare state itself.

*

If this is not enough to make Stieg's novels different from most other Swedish fiction, there is also Lisbeth Salander, his heroine, as well as most of the other women in the books, who virtually all differ drastically from the way women are generally depicted in Sweden. Apart from Salander, recurring female characters include Erika Berger, a magazine and newspaper editor, living in an open marriage which allows her sexual relations with a man who is not her spouse; Annika Giannini, a brilliant trial lawyer; policewomen like Sonja Modig and Monica Figuerola, expert fighters; Miriam Wu, Lisbeth Salander's lover, a fetishist performance artist. And at stage centre, Salander herself, a woman totally oblivious of any expectations placed on her by her surroundings, which is perhaps the most challenging stand one could possibly take, not least in Sweden.

Much has been made of the fact that Salander refuses to be a victim. To that extent, she reflects the consensus view of Swedish feminism: women are almost inevitably victimized, but must refuse to succumb; the feminist tenet is that women must organize to empower each other and to reject victimization. However, the point in Stieg Larsson's novels is that Lisbeth Salander refuses not only to be a victim, but also to seek fulfilment in a collective stand or seek redress through institutionalized means. When wronged, she will avenge herself. She has no interest in being nurturing, and rejects the notion that this is a role natural to women. She has no interest in analysing or "working on" her relationships and rejects the notion that this is how women are supposed to be. She distrusts the authorities, refuses to complain and instead acts on her own to gain and guard her rights. She rejects the consensus doctrine and trusts only in her own judgment and morality. She rejects the notion that women should dress and act to please men and instead dresses and acts to please herself. She rejects both the heterosexual norm and the idea of lesbian exclusivity, and seeks erotic fulfilment with those individuals she is attracted to, regardless of gender. She is, in short, the nightmare of all doctrines, all consensus thinkers, all moralists and all politicians: the individual complete unto herself, with neither need of nor respect for authority, traditions, public opinion, established morality or accepted behaviour.

As has been pointed out by Swedish professor Eva Lundgren, Stieg Larsson was well aware of how radical a break a protagonist of this kind was with Swedish tradition, and so in the first of his novels he "softens" the impact of Lisbeth Salander by providing her with a diagnosis: she is presented as suffering from Asberger's syndrome, and thus as a woman lacking in empathy. To Swedish readers, this would in a sense be a relief; they are now free to accept Salander as depicted, while at the same time being allowed to feel sorry for her. She is no "real woman", as women always are empathetic, but since her lack is due to illness, it is acceptable and she can be viewed with sympathy. However, in the third novel, Stieg Larsson withdraws this safety net. In the court hearing, the diagnosis is now nullified. Lisbeth Salander had a difficult childhood, a sadistic father, a battered mother, but was not ill: she is a normal human being, acting and reacting in ways which must therefore be accepted as reasonable and sane, given her circumstances. Given the consistency of Stieg's portrayal of Lisbeth through the three novels, by this time most of his readers will be willing to accept this. But in doing so, they also accept the possibility of a normal woman who refuses to accede to even a single one of the traditional stereotyped perceptions of how women should look, act, react, feel or respond. And this, I would submit, is precisely the point.

It is also fundamentally un-Swedish, as the reigning superlative in Swedish behaviour, thinking and normation is, and for a long time has been, the notion of *lagom* – a word lacking an exact equivalent in most languages, but meaning "just enough", neither too much nor too little; what you should expect and what others will deem your fair share. Lisbeth Salander is not content with that; she wants and expects to live her life according to her own ideas, beliefs, morality and resources, regardless of what anyone else may feel or think about it. And in that sense, and as she is also resourceful, strong, intelligent and willing to act, she is a heroine. But, and this point can hardly be overstressed, the consensual idea is that as the benign welfare state will provide a safe, problem-free existence for all, individual heroism is not only unnecessary but actually detrimental. To the extent that the world, or an individual, needs to be saved, doing it is the province of government (or, as Swedes would prefer to say, "public" or "collective") action; for an individual to assume that responsibility is not only presumptuous, but implies putting her individual interpretation above that of others, which is worse than presumptuous: it reeks of anarchism.

And of course Lisbeth Salander *is* an anarchist heroine, which is, if that is possible, even more un-Swedish than an individualist hero. In a consensus-driven society, the unrepentant individual is always suspect, and the anarchist is a threat. It is a tribute to Stieg Larsson's storytelling powers that, despite this, he managed to make his anarchist individualist heroine palatable, and loved, by millions of Swedes. And, incidentally, perhaps their acceptance of Lisbeth Salander is also a sign that Swedes are finally getting ready to leave their Castle in the Air behind.

In early 2010, a weird debate briefly dominated the Swedish media.

First, there was Kurdo Baksi's rather self-serving memoir, called *Min vän Stieg Larsson* [*Stieg Larsson, My Friend*, MacLehose Press, 2010]. It was the first book about Stieg, and in the course of an interview for it Baksi claimed that he was in fact a better writer than Stieg had been, and that during their acquaintance he had often heavily edited Stieg's writing before publication. Shortly after the book was published, Anders Hellberg, a journalist employed by Sweden's largest daily, *Dagens Nyheter*, wrote an article in which he claimed that he had worked alongside Stieg Larsson at the T.T. news agency up until 1981, and that he often had to rewrite Stieg's captions for the graphics he drew, since Stieg's writing was "simply bad". Accordingly, Hellberg claimed, Stieg Larsson could not possibly have written the three *Millennium* novels; someone else had to have either written them or, at least, extensively edited and rewritten them.

This claim is not only unsubstantiated but absurd enough to be laughable.

Stieg Larsson wrote continuously from his earliest teens until his death. His writing from as early as 1972 until his death is in print and available for analysis. Yes, over the years he learned to write better. No, he never became an impressive or sensitive stylist. But most importantly, there is nothing in the three *Millennium* novels that disproves that they could have been written by the man who wrote immature short stories in mimeographed fanzines in 1972, who wrote humorous essays in other fanzines in 1976, who wrote book reviews and essays in 1980, books about right-wing extremists in 1990 and analyses of violence against women in 2004.

What Anders Hellberg suggested in his original article was that Eva Gabrielsson must have either written or extensively edited the novels. Eva Gabrielsson has repeatedly denied this, though at the same time noting that she did, indeed, have an impact on the books. Others commenting on this, both in Sweden and abroad, have seemed uncertain as to how Eva's comments should be interpreted. But I suspect that this is simply because these writers did not know Stieg and Eva.

Eva was not only in the general sense Stieg's partner for more than thirty years, but much more importantly his partner in virtually everything. I have seldom met any couple so intensely and joyfully a constant part of each other's lives. This essay is primarily about Stieg Larsson, but it would be sadly lacking if I did not at least at some point stress that almost everything I have talked about Stieg doing, Eva did as well and in her own right. She as well as Stieg was active in science-fiction fandom, in politics, in writing. They compared notes, co-wrote things, discussed with each other and, together, with everyone else. At parties they never exhibited the common behaviour of couples who go their separate ways, after which the man talks to other men and the woman to other women; they stayed together, discussed together with men and women alike. It is true that they had different specializations – Eva is an architect. But they shared all, worked and functioned as a team, and were inseparable for as long as Stieg lived.

The first *Millennium* novel was begun during 2002, when Stieg and Eva rented a summer cottage by the sea and Eva was working on a non-fiction architecture-related book of her own. I would take for granted that as they progressed, both their books were constantly read by both, discussed and commented on; I would also take for granted that in a very real sense, Stieg was present in the book Eva was writing, and Eva in the book Stieg was writing, as in the two that followed. Again, I would also take for granted that they had been present in each other's writings constantly since the mid '70s, when they began living together. And even though Hellberg's assertion that Stieg could not have written his novels alone thus in one sense had some truth in it – for without Eva I suspect that much of what Stieg wrote throughout his life would have been different – in another sense it remains flatly nonsensical. I do not have the slightest doubt that Stieg wrote the *Millennium* novels in exactly the same way he wrote most of his work: by himself, in an ongoing creative partnership with Eva

Stieg Larsson's strength as a writer was neither impeccable prose nor stylistic experimentation. His prose was not impeccable and his style was pedestrian. He was a journalistic writer, prone to repetition, the occasional misplaced word, the occasional misspelling, the occasional pedantic enumeration. The vividness of his novels is not linguistic but a matter of evocativeness: his clear visualization of characters, his sheer storytelling talent. If anything, his novels are an illustration of the idea that a good enough storyteller is able to transcend the limitations of his style. Praising Stieg's novels, Peruvian novelist and perennial Nobel candidate Mario Vargas Llosa has said that they remind him of his childhood reading of works such as Alexandre Dumas' *The Man in the Iron Mask*. To be good, Vargas Llosa said in *El País*, a novel need not be perfect. And in fact Dumas, like Stieg Larsson, was an indifferent writer, as good writing is defined and discussed. Which actually does not much matter. Occasionally, a great writer is also a great storyteller, and this makes authors like Virginia Woolf, Vladimir Nabokov, Angela Carter and Joseph Conrad immortal. But more often the writer with perfect pitch and a talent for stylistic innovation is not a gifted storyteller, and perhaps sadly this will make her or his work quickly forgotten. While the great storyteller is fairly often indifferent to stylistic finesse, which seems seldom to bother readers, and this is as true of C. S. Forester, Sir Arthur Conan Doyle or Dame Agatha Christie as it is of Stieg Larsson.

Early November 2004 was almost uniquely warm for that time of year in Sweden. On Wednesday, November 10, I was queuing at the ice-cream van with my two youngest children when my mobile rang. It was Eva Gabrielsson. "Stieg is dead," she said, and my children tell me that I was speechless and turned very pale.

On November 9, Stieg had begun the day as he most often did, by waking sometime after noon, having written through the night and probably falling asleep at six or seven in the morning. He would have broken his fast on black coffee and a cigarette or two, packed his work computer and whatever research material he wanted to bring in his shoulder bag, then walked to the *Expo* offices. As the foundation, as well as its staff, was constantly under threat from the various individuals and organizations it exposed, the office was housed on the top floor of an apartment building; its door sign carried only a neutral family name. On that day the elevator did not work, and Stieg had to walk up the stairs to the office. When he arrived, he was pale and short of breath. One of his colleagues was frightened by his appearance and asked if he should call a doctor. "Perhaps you should," Stieg said. "I don't feel well." He collapsed to the floor. While trying to revive him in the ambulance, the paramedics asked for the year, his name, his age. According to what they said, his only and last words were, "I'm fifty, damn it!"

I had last spoken to Stieg perhaps a week earlier. Our last e-mails were exchanged around the middle of October. And I had last met him a little over three months before, when he and Eva along with Eva's sister were travelling around southern Sweden in search of a small cottage to buy and spent an afternoon, evening and night with me and my family. Stieg had signed the contract offered him by Norstedts and would get an advance against royalties which he hoped would enable him and Eva to buy a small place to spend their free time, and where he could sometimes go to write without any disturbances. We talked about this, about his novels, about his recent anthology on violence against women, and he said that he looked forward to many more similar nights. The moon was red and full, the night was warm, we had dinner outside and stayed at the table, talking, until the small hours of the morning. The whisky was good, the smoke from our cigarettes kept the mosquitoes at bay and Stieg was as full of life, opinions, good humour and optimism as ever. "A place down here would be wonderful," he said. "I'll finally be able to afford to take it easy sometimes, to just write what I feel like."

He was right about many things. I wish he had been right about that as well.

John-Henri Holmberg worked for many years as a book editor, publisher and translator, and is author of and contributor to books on science fiction, fantasy, psychological suspense and twentieth-century cinema. He is a member of the Swedish Crime Fiction Academy and as a hobby publishes Sweden's only professional science-fiction magazine, Nova.

THE STIEG LARSSON PHENOMENON

Svante Weyler

As I write this, in June 2010, tourists are taking Stockholm by storm. My office is in a stone building in Gamla Stan, the Old Town, and I am watching people's curious gaze exploring the narrow medieval alleys. Are they discovering the real Sweden here among all these old buildings? The land which is often called the most modern country in the world?

At the same time, in a different part of the city, groups of tourists are retracing the steps of Stieg Larsson and the characters in his novels – the books that are being read just now on every beach and in every bedroom all over the world. There is not much sign of Sweden's medieval past here, but plenty of the welfare state that we like to call "the people's home": substantial apartments for upright citizens. I know exactly where these groups generally stop to gaze up at the windows above. I used to live more or less next door to Lisbeth in the hilly Söder district of Stockholm. Nowadays it is far too expensive for ordinary people to live there.

We Stockholmers are quite fascinated by these groups of dedicated Stieg Larsson enthusiasts. Mainly because we are flattered by the attention he has generated. You could say that Stieg Larsson was one of us. That is what we call ordinary Swedes. A few ordinary Swedes have become world-famous: Björn Borg, Birgit Nilsson, Benny Andersson. And now Stieg Larsson.

And then, of course, we ask ourselves just what are these people looking for. Are they simply trying to pin down locations in the novels, or are they after something more than that? Are they looking for Sweden? For Swedes? Do they want to know whether Lisbeth Salander was just an ordinary Swedish woman, or was she unique? Do Swedish men really hate women? Is it really possible that Mikael Blomkvist could not only collect his child from nursery school, but also pull his full weight when it came to dealing with the laundry and doing the washing up? In short: is Stieg Larsson telling the truth, or is he making it all up?

Swedish crime novels are today achieving unprecedented success in all parts of the world – and it is not only Stieg Larsson. But the fact is that even if he has a lot in common with the biggest names in this field – Sjöwall and Wahlöö, Henning Mankell, Åsa Larsson, Åke Edwardson, Håkan Nesser – there is even more that distinguishes him from them. What they all share is a nostalgic, usually left-of-centre view of the way in which Swedish society has developed over the last thirty years. The basic premise is simple: things were better in the old days. This is proved by soaring crime rates, a new sense of insecurity: the people's home is, slowly but surely, crumbling.

It is very doubtful if this is a true picture of Sweden, but what is perhaps more important is that it is a view which even Swedish readers accept, and they seem to have an insatiable appetite for such writing.

The image of Sweden as a lost paradise contains several paradoxes. In all international comparative studies, Sweden emerges as a relatively peaceful country with minimal levels of corruption, both in the business and financial worlds as well as in politics. We do have Hell's Angels, of course, like everybody else, and cars are occasionally set on fire in our suburbs, but nevertheless, it is clear that the image of Sweden which emerges in Swedish crime novels is not a true reflection of the actual situation. But then, why should literature worry about being a true reflection? After all, it is by no means sure that Inspector Maigret was a typical French police officer. Or that James Bond would really have been given a job with M.I.6.

All Swedish readers would probably agree that Mikael Blomkvist is somebody you might well bump into at the corner shop; but we have never met anybody like Lisbeth Salander. We have taken her to our hearts even so. What attracts us is not the truth, but the possible.

Perhaps that is what we should whisper in the ears of the Italians and the English and the Spaniards and the Germans and all the other Larsson readers wandering about in the Söder district of Stockholm. It is not true, it is merely possible.

So much for what they have in common. But what differentiates them is more important: no other Swedish crime writer in recent years has placed as much importance on the development of the plot as Stieg Larsson. In a way that makes him the least Swedish of them all, for his narrative method is based on exceptional knowledge of the Anglo-Saxon tradition.

Perhaps this is one of the explanations of his world-wide success: a unique combination of traditional, Anglo-Saxon narrative technique, and a comprehensive knowledge of the often hidden, murky depths of Swedish society.

Was this all clear from the very start? Did we have a clear sense of what we had been presented with?

I have told the story a thousand times. It is not especially long or complicated.

Another of the Norstedts authors phoned me. He said he was working on a magazine together with a journalist who had recently written three crime novels. Would I like to take a look at them? Of course.

Stieg Larsson turned up at the publishing house with two of the novels in a plastic carrier bag. I thanked him, and promised to read them quickly. I only had one question: how come that he had not shown these novels to anybody until now? He replied casually that he had the feeling they might be quite good, so he wanted to finish them in peace and quiet.

We read the books just as quickly as we had said we would, and had no hesitation in coming to a decision. We realized that we had a unique opportunity. Normally a publisher has only one novel to launch, and then can do no more than keep his fingers crossed and hope that the first one was not a flash in the pan, but that subsequent books, as yet unwritten, will live up to the promise of their predecessor. But in this case we had no grounds for such qualms: we knew already that they would. Instead we had a different problem: how could we manage to convince Stieg Larsson that these books were among the best we had ever seen? Was he only interested in the money, or were there other considerations as far as he was concerned?

We made him an offer that was unordinarily big, but by no means astronomical. He reacted exactly as I had thought and hoped he would. "This shows me that you believe in my books," he said, "and also that I will be able to make a living by continuing to write novels. So, let's get on with it."

The same approach as before. The faith we had in him was just as important as the money, or so I interpreted it in any case.

A few months later, after a short summer and half an autumn, he was dead. The first text I wrote about him was an obituary. What do you write about an author you have met only a handful of times, whose novels have not yet been published but who has nevertheless aroused a great deal of attention? It is like writing about a star that died out even before it had appeared in the night sky.

After having worked with and mixed with authors for half my life, I know by experience that a writer feels two different kinds of happiness. The first one is the only thing an author can be sure about: the joy induced by the actual writing process. The other involves his or her relationship with readers.

Afterwards – a long time afterwards – it is always recognized that the first kind was the more important. That is something I tried to console Stieg's family, his friends and myself with when we assembled to celebrate his life after his idiotic death. I like to think that the happiness writing bestows is so all-consuming because it is linked with freedom. Before anybody else knows that you are writing, or what you are writing, you are free to write whatever you like. Later on you have to cope with other people's comments, the expectations of your readers and the hopes of your publisher. This combination can also bring happiness, but it can just as easily bring disappointment and pressure.

I believe that the relaxed attitude I was not the only one to discern in Stieg Larsson during our brief meetings was an expression of the sense of joyful freedom he derived from his secret work at the computer.

The law does not take emotions into consideration. Perhaps that is why we have laws.

For a short time after Stieg Larsson's death I found myself at the centre of a complicated argument about how his estate ought to be distributed. In one sense the argument was not complicated at all: Swedish inheritance laws are crystal clear. As Stieg Larsson was not married, his partner Eva Gabrielsson could only count on the very limited bounty the law prescribed. The rest of the estate – a portion that at the time did not seem nearly as substantial as it has now become – went to his parents; and since his mother was already dead, her share passed to Stieg's brother. This is the reason, which many observers find difficult to accept, why all aspects of Stieg Larsson's writings are now controlled by his father and his brother rather than the woman with whom he shared so much of his life, and who watched the novels being created at the computer on the kitchen table she shared with the author. At the time, none of us could possibly have dreamed of the staggering sums the royalties would involve. If we had been able to, discussions between the family and Stieg Larsson's partner might well have turned out differently.

What role did Norstedts have to play in all this? Formally speaking, none at all. The publisher had and still has nothing to do with arguments concerning the destiny of the author's income as we were the counterpart in the contract; but from a moral point of view we were deeply involved. We tried to mediate regarding emotions and points of view between the two "sides" in the hope of achieving a more equitable outcome than that prescribed by the law, an aspiration clearly hoped for by all parties. I do not know if we could have done anything differently at the time, or if it might be possible to do something different now. All I do know is that it is incredibly difficult to interpret the possible wishes of a deceased person without a factual documentary basis. It is difficult for a publishing house, and also difficult for the next of kin. All one can do is to try one's best. Will it be possible to reach an agreement? Only if there is a genuine desire to reach an agreement.

Death delivers a final verdict, and like the law, it never takes feelings into account.

As I write the newspapers are full of speculation as to who will play the part of Lisbeth Salander in the American version of the films. And which of all the chocolate-box charmers will have the pleasure of playing the ladykiller Mikael B. We ought to be proud of that, because in normal circumstances being noticed in Hollywood is a bit like being ennobled by Queen Elizabeth. Money talks. Big money talks more.

But in fact all the fuss is completely unnecessary. Lisbeth S. exists already – in three versions: Stieg Larsson's, every individual reader's, and Noomi Rapace's brilliant interpretation of this melancholy, angry young woman.

And every time you look her in the eye, you understand the real answer to the question of what turned Stieg Larsson's three Swedish novels into a matter of concern to the whole wide world: Lisbeth Salander.

It is for her sake that tourists flock to Stockholm. But they will never set eyes on her. Not because she does not exist, but because she does not like tourists.

Translated by Laurie Thompson

Svante Weyler was Publishing Director of Norstedts and a cultural journalist. He now runs his own publishing house, Weyler Förlag, in Stockholm.